DRIVING STANDARDS AGE[illegible]

# THE Bus and Coach Driving Manual

DRIVING SKILLS

INSTRUCTOR

S.J. McGOUGH.

London: The Stationery Office

Written by the Publications Unit of the Driving Standards Agency
Graphics by Vicky Squires

Published by The Stationery Office Limited



First edition Crown copyright 1995

ISBN 0 11 551784 7

British Library Catalogue in Publication Data
A CIP catalogue record for this book is available from the British Library

Other titles in the Driving Skills series

*The Official Theory Test for Car Drivers and Motorcyclists*
*The Official Theory Test for Large Vehicle Drivers*
*The Driving Test*
*The Driving Manual*
*The Motorcycling Manual*
*The Goods Vehicle Driving Manual*
*Driving Skills: The Theory Test and Beyond* (CD-ROM)

The Driving Standards Agency (DSA) would like to thank the following for their assistance

- The staff of the Driving Standards Agency
- The Traffic Director for London
- The National Federation of Bus Users
- The staff of the Department of Transport and its Agencies

# ABOUT THE DRIVING STANDARDS AGENCY

The Driving Standards Agency (DSA) is an Executive Agency of the Department of Transport. You'll see its logo at test centres.

The aim of DSA is to promote road safety through the advancement of driving standards.

**DSA**

- Conducts practical driving tests for drivers or riders of cars, motorcycles, lorries, buses and other vehicles
- Plans, maintains and supervises the theory test for drivers or riders of cars, motorcycles, lorries and buses
- Controls the register of Approved Driving Instructors (ADIs)
- Supervises Compulsory Basic Training (CBT) courses for motorcyclists
- Aims to provide a high-quality service to its customers

# CONTENTS

## PART FIVE The PCV Driving Test



## PART SIX Additional Information

This book provides detailed professional guidance for the safe driving of buses and coaches. As the driver of a vehicle carrying passengers you must accept responsibility for their safety. Whether you drive a minibus with eight passengers or a double-decker coach with 88 people, each one is relying on you to look after them.

The starting point for a professional driver is having the correct attitude. You should set an example through courtesy and consideration, and make allowances for the mistakes of other drivers. A professional driver will have a sound knowledge of driving theory coupled with the ability to apply that theory in an expert manner.

Changes to the driving test are the result of new legislation imposed by the European Commission (second EC directive). These have been implemented in the interest of road safety. The changes are included in this book and will help PCV drivers to keep up to date with the new legislation.

This book provides an officially recommended syllabus for learning how to drive a bus or coach, plus a structured approach to training that should help you to progress to a professional standard. Studying *The Bus and Coach Driving Manual* will help you to achieve a better understanding of the skills and attitudes that combine to make for higher driving standards.

*Robin Cummins*
**The Chief Driving Examiner**
**Driving Standards Agency**

*The Bus and Coach Driving Manual* is about driving the many different types and sizes of passenger carrying vehicles (PCVs) – buses, coaches and minibuses. It's written in six easy-to-read parts in the established Driving Standards Agency (DSA) style, which includes plenty of illustrations with clear and straightforward instruction and advice.

## PART ONE Getting Started

PCV drivers need to be thoroughly professional in their approach. This part of the book helps you to understand the range of knowledge that a new PCV driver needs to acquire. It also shows what skills need to be learned in order to drive competently and safely. How to obtain a provisional PCV licence is explained, together with the essential differences between driving cars and larger vehicles. The importance of the correct attitude to driving, in addition to the differing vehicle characteristics, is also covered.

## PART TWO Limits and Regulations

PCV drivers need to know the legal limits that affect their vehicle and their driving. These limits are extensive and are explained here in full.

## PART THREE Driving Skills

This part of the book gives advice on professional driving, as well as driving in various weather conditions, at night and on motorways. It also deals with accidents and breakdowns.

## PART FOUR Test Preparation

This section contains the officially recommended syllabus for the PCV driving test. There's also detailed guidance on how to prepare and apply for the test.

## PART FIVE The PCV Driving Test

All the aspects of the driving test are covered in this part of the book. The test requirements, the skills you should show and the faults you should avoid are explained fully. Action you can take upon receiving your test results is also considered.

## PART SIX Additional Information

DSA services, including the complaints guide and compensation code, are all included in this part. Useful addresses and other helpful information can also be found here.

Reading this book should help you to appreciate the principles of driving PCVs and lead you to become a safer driver.

# PART ONE GETTING STARTED

This part provides the basic information that you'll need to know and understand before you embark on professional training for driving PCVs.

## The topics covered

- Getting started
- The PCV driver
- Attitude
- Driving forces
- Types of PCVs
- Vehicle braking and steering systems

## Applying for your licence

In order to drive PCVs you must apply to the Driver and Vehicle Licensing Agency (DVLA), Swansea, for provisional PCV entitlement to be added to your full car (category B) licence, unless you've held the entitlement before. You must not drive a PCV until you've received your licence with the proper category added.

To be issued a licence to drive PCVs you must

- Be at or above the minimum age for the category of vehicle you intend to drive – see the relevant table in Part Six
- Have a full category B licence – you can't take a driving test on a bus before passing a car test
- Meet the medical requirements
- Pay the fee

You can obtain a driving licence application form (D1) from

- Post offices
- Traffic Area Offices
- Vehicle registration offices (VROs)
- DVLA Customer Enquiries Unit, Swansea SA6 7JL

Read carefully the notes that accompany the form and fill in all the relevant parts. The form may have to be returned to you and there could be a delay in issuing your licence if you leave anything out. If you need advice about completing the form ring the enquiry number for DVLA listed at the back of this book.

Send the completed application form and

- Your category B licence, or provisional car driving licence and a valid driving test pass certificate (form D10)
- A completed medical report form (D4), signed by a doctor
- The appropriate fee

to the DVLA, Swansea SA99 1BR. The current fees and ways to pay are listed on the application form.

### Automatic transmission

If your category B licence is restricted to automatic vehicles you can only drive a PCV with an automatic gearbox. Vehicles with fully automatic, semi-automatic, pneumo-cyclic, electronically controlled or pre-select gearboxes with a gear-change pedal are all classified as automatic.

If a vehicle has a clutch pedal it's classified as having a manual gearbox. To drive a PCV with a manual gearbox you'll have to pass a test in a car or a lorry with a manual gearbox.

## Second EC directive

Changes resulting from the implementation of the second EC directive mean that since 1 January 1997 all new drivers wishing to drive PCVs or large goods vehicles (LGVs) will first have to pass the theory test for PCVs/LGVs before taking the practical driving test. Between 1 January and 30 June 1997 an interim arrangement allows the tests to be taken in either order. If the practical test is passed first, drivers then have six months to pass the theory test. If the theory test is passed first, drivers have two years in which to pass the practical test.

Drivers who already hold a full car licence (category B) won't have to take the theory test to drive minibuses with less than nine passenger seats. However, to obtain a category D1 licence to drive either a minibus or midibus with 9–16 passenger seats a driver must have a full category B licence and pass the theory test before applying to take the practical driving test. Similarly, to obtain a category D licence to drive a minibus, midibus, coach, single- or double-decker bus with more than 16 passenger seats a driver must have a full category B licence and pass the theory test before applying to take the practical driving test.

### Additional notes

- A category D licence is required to drive articulated buses (described in the UK as 'bendi-buses')
- It won't be necessary to first obtain a category D1 or D1 + E licence before applying for a category D test
- If a trailer with a maximum permitted weight of more than 750kg is to be towed, a category B + E, D1 + E or D + E licence may be required, as appropriate. A trailer weighing less than 750kg may be towed by any of the vehicles in these licence categories
- Passengers may NOT be carried in any trailer

If you're unsure of the category of licence entitlement that you need, see the charts in Part Six at the back of this book.

## Eyesight requirements

All drivers, for whatever category of vehicle, must be able to read a number plate in good daylight at 20.5 metres (67 feet). If glasses or contact lenses are needed to do this they must be worn while driving.

In addition, any applicant for a bus licence must have a visual acuity of at least

- 6/9 in the better eye
- 6/12 in the other eye

when wearing glasses or contact lenses, if needed. There must also be normal vision in both eyes (defined as a 120° field) and no evidence of double vision (diplopia). Satisfactory uncorrected visual acuity is also required of applicants.

Any applicant who has uncorrected acuity of less than 3/60 in both eyes (when tested separately) won't be able to meet the required standard. Your doctor will use the standard Snellen test card to test your eyesight. If you only have eyesight in one eye you must declare this on form D1.

An applicant or licence-holder who held a PCV/LGV licence before 1 March 1992 but whose eyesight doesn't meet the required standard will no longer qualify for a licence. So-called 'grandfather rights' are no longer permitted. Further information about the standard for such an applicant can be obtained from the DVLA Drivers' Medical Unit.

## Medical examination and form D4

Consult your doctor first if you have any doubts about your fitness. In any case, if this is your first application for PCV entitlement a medical examination must be carried out by a doctor.

You'll need to send a medical report (form D4) off with your application. You'll also need to send a report if you're renewing your PCV licence and you're aged 45 or over, unless you've already sent one to DVLA during the last 12 months.

In order to complete form D4 you'll need to undergo a medical examination. You should only complete the applicant details and declaration (Section 8 on the form) when you're with your doctor at the time of the examination. Your doctor has to witness you doing this. The other sections on the form will be completed by your doctor. The medical report will cover

- Vision
- Nervous system
- Diabetes mellitus
- Psychiatric illness
- General health
- Cardiac health
- Medical practitioner details

After the medical examination, study the notes on pages 1 and 2 of the form. Remove these pages before sending in your application and keep them for future reference.

The medical examination isn't available free under National Health rules. Your doctor is entitled to charge the current fee for this medical examination, which you'll be responsible for. It can't be recovered from DVLA, and the fee isn't refundable if your application is refused.

The completed form must be received by DVLA within four months of your doctor signing it.

### Medical standards

You may be refused a PCV driving licence if you suffer from any of the following

- Liability to epilepsy/seizure
- Diabetes requiring insulin (unless you held a licence on 1 April 1991 and the Traffic Commissioner who issued that licence had knowledge of your condition)
- Visual defects (see eyesight requirements on p. 7)
- Heart disorders
- Persistent high blood pressure
- Strokes/unconscious lapses within the last five years
- Any disorder causing vertigo within the last two years
- Severe head injury, with serious continuing after-effects, or major brain surgery
- Parkinson's disease, multiple sclerosis or other chronic nervous disorders likely to affect the use of the limbs
- Mental disorders
- Alcohol/drug problems
- Serious difficulty in communicating by telephone in an emergency
- Visual field defects

An applicant or licence-holder failing to meet the epilepsy, diabetes or eyesight regulations must by law be refused a licence.

## Professional standards

To drive a bus, coach or minibus you need to have the right skills and attitude. For a start, you must appreciate the differences between driving larger and smaller vehicles. Some of these aspects will be obvious from the moment you first start to drive a larger vehicle. Other features will only become apparent as you continue to drive.

The essential factor to recognise is that forward planning is vital in order to drive a bus, coach or minibus safely. The comfort and safety of your passengers must always be your primary concern. Your company's good name will be at stake if you don't take care of customers. In addition, you must show responsibility towards all other road users.

It's best to apply the professional driving techniques described in this book. Remember, you must never allow safety to be put at risk.

**No risk is ever justified.**

To become a professional bus, coach or minibus driver you'll need a thorough knowledge of the regulations that apply to your work. A comprehensive knowledge of *The Highway Code*, including the meaning of traffic signs and road markings (especially those that indicate restrictions for large vehicles), will also be needed.

Most importantly, you'll need to have a high level of driving skill. The **way** you drive is vitally important.

- Drive properly, and your passengers will arrive safely at their destination
- Drive carelessly or dangerously, and you risk the safety of your passengers and other road users

If you act hastily you risk endangering others. You need to constantly assess all the factors that might affect your task, and plan your actions early.

When a bus or coach is involved in an accident it's bound to lead to damage, injury or loss of life. As a professional driver you have a part to play in making sure accidents don't happen.

Around 90% of road accidents are due to human error. High-quality training should help you to avoid making such errors and reduce the risk of you becoming involved in accidents.

Sometimes accidents are due to the mechanical failure of vehicle components. The way you drive can affect the life of these components. Drivers who demonstrate a high degree of expertise cut the risk of accidents happening. So, be responsible for driving your vehicle safely and sensibly at all times.

## Caring for passengers

Your job is to deliver your passengers to their destinations

- Safely
- On time
- Efficiently
- Courteously

Caring for your passengers is as important a part of PCV driving as are the individual driving skills. As the driver, you're responsible for your passengers. They'll look upon you as the acknowledged expert and representative of the company. How well you perform this role is a measure of your professionalism.

Many companies have rules governing standards of behaviour from both you and passengers. These are in addition to the more general statutory laws that drivers of PCVs must obey. Make sure that you know the rules and enforce them when necessary.

At some point you'll also find yourself driving to a timetable. This can exert a pressure on you to rush. Resist the temptation to hurry and don't become impatient.

### Customer care

- Be on the lookout for passengers. Those waiting might not be able to see or hear the bus coming
- Eliminate gaps from the kerb. Many passengers find it difficult to board or get off the bus if it pulls up too far away from the kerb. Stop well in to help them
- Look directly at each passenger when you speak. It may make a world of difference to some of your customers
- Give passengers time to get seated before you move off. A few extra seconds here add very little to journey times but make a huge difference to some customers

## Professional service

Operators often publicise journeys as being

- Comfortable
- Convenient
- Fast
- Trouble-free

Drivers are important in delivering this standard of service.

Consider this example: Two almost identical vehicles from different companies operating the same route are at the bus stop together. There are 30 people in the queue. Six get on the first bus and 24 on the second one. The second one is behind but still manages to pull away first, entirely as a result of good planning.

The driver of the second bus keeps 5 and 10p coins separately in her cash bag so that she can give change to passengers quickly. Having left enough room to manoeuvre clear, she's able to pull away quicker – still smiling.

The other driver is chatting to his friend at the front of the bus. Passengers have to ask twice for their tickets. He fumbles around for the correct change, grumbling, 'Have you got anything smaller?'

During your training you should travel on the type of vehicles that you'll be driving. Notice how the drivers treat you as a passenger. Learn from the best.

## Passengers with special needs

*'If someone smiles and takes the money with a little bit of patience it makes the world of difference.'*

*'Just speaking carefully, looking at the person and giving them attention – not feeling rushed – matters a lot. The feeling that you're holding up a queue of people is a very anxiety-producing situation.'*

These are comments from passengers about their local bus service. They're the sort of people you might carry every day – regular customers, in fact. Yet both of them have a problem that may be hard to recognise: they're disabled.

Some disabilities are very obvious. A person carrying a white stick, a long white cane or accompanied by a guide dog is visually impaired. If the stick has red rings painted on it they also have impaired hearing. It's also easy to see that someone with crutches, a walking frame or any other aid to movement has a disability – perhaps only temporarily.

Your actions towards such passengers will directly influence the quality of their travel experience. Remember, showing a little consideration goes a long way with most people – whether they have special needs or not.

Your personal experience may include helping people who, every day of their lives, face challenges to their mobility. If so, you'll be familiar with their problems. If not, try to imagine what assistance *you* would like if you were in their position.

Try to be patient and considerate. Always respect their wishes: disabled people want to retain their independence. If someone tells you they can manage – let them. But be prepared to offer help if they appear to need it, or ask for it.You'll have your own problems to cope with – such as trying to keep to time, busy traffic conditions, inconsiderate behaviour by other road users. But you should do your best to offer courtesy and a smooth ride to those with special needs. Also, think about the everyday problems faced by people trying to manage with children, pushchairs or shopping trolleys.

### The blind and partially sighted

More than 200,000 people in the UK are visually impaired. Only a small proportion are totally blind, but you may not be able to tell by their appearance. Visually handicapped people often depend on their local bus service for mobility. And remember, most partially sighted people find it hard to read a destination display or timetable.

*'There's a problem of explaining that we can't see very well ... we want to do as much as we can for ourselves and just be helped with the tiny bit that we can't do...'*

### The deaf and hearing-impaired

*'I usually ask the fare and, if I don't hear how much it is, sometimes I bluff and just offer £1 and hope to get the right change. If the bus driver seems to be a pleasant, approachable person I don't mind asking him to repeat it, but some drivers are under pressure and appear not to be aware of you or don't look at your face...'*

It's common courtesy to look at people when you speak to them. Just doing that will allow most deaf or hearing-impaired people to understand you. Good communication also saves time.

### Physical disabilities

People with arthritis, stiff joints, artificial limbs or conditions such as multiple sclerosis often put up with extra pain (and the impatience of other passengers) rather than ask for extra consideration on a bus. For them, courtesy and a smooth ride are important.

*'Nobody wants to shout to the rest of the world "I am having trouble", but if the driver could just wait until you're sitting down before they pulled away...'*

*'If letting the clutch out or moving away is done too violently it hurts every inch of the way...'*

*'If the driver was to go round corners a little more slowly it would probably be less painful...'*

**Lifts, ramps and 'kneeling' buses**
Make sure that you're thoroughly trained in the safe use of passenger lifts, ramps and securing devices. If you drive a vehicle fitted with this equipment, never let untrained people operate lifts, etc. Watch out for the safety of others at all times.

Some buses are equipped with air or hydraulic systems that allow the step level to be raised and lowered. These 'kneeling' buses improve access for disabled and elderly passengers. It's essential that you're thoroughly trained in the use of such systems and are aware of the principles of safe operation.

## Learning disabilities

Customers with learning disabilities may appear fit and active, but they may also find bus travel a special problem and a challenge. It may be hard for them to understand other people or to make themselves understood. Also, any unexpected problems can sometimes produce a sense of panic.

Those with learning disabilities are increasingly being encouraged to go out to work, to go shopping or visit friends. With patience and understanding you can contribute towards their confidence and sense of achievement.

## Be a credit

There's a lot of competition among operators for passengers. Such competition helps to ensure that high-quality services are available. However, competition also means that operators need to have tight cost controls to ensure efficient and effective use of their resources. But cutting corners on safety isn't acceptable and could be a recipe for disaster. Remember, safety should be your **first** priority.

- You must not drive a vehicle with a serious defect
- If you're delayed, do your best to make up time but don't speed or take risks
- Obstructing and 'racing' another operator's vehicles is inexcusable

Courtesy and consideration are the hallmarks of a professional driver. Both you and your company, not to mention your profession, will be on display every time you drive. Therefore, you should show a good example of skill, courtesy and tolerance. Be a credit to yourself, your company and your profession, and aim for the highest standards.

## Appropriate behaviour

Your role in customer care is important, but you also need to consider your attitude whilst driving.

The sheer size, noise and appearance of a typical PCV can appear intimidating to cyclists, pedestrians and even car drivers. When a bus or coach seems to be driven in an aggressive way, other road users can feel really threatened.

The general public tend to see the bus or coach driver either as

- A skilful professional who manoeuvres a large vehicle in difficult spaces and delivers passengers safely to their destination, or
- An impatient person determined to make other road users, and his or her passengers, do precisely what he or she wants

A PCV driver should create the best possible image by setting a good example for others to follow.

Driving large vehicles can be very enjoyable – even more so when you can be proud that you're doing it well.

## Tailgating

Tailgating involves travelling dangerously close behind another vehicle, at speed, and only a few feet apart. This often happens on motorways.

Not only are tailgating and driving in close convoy with other PCVs bad driving habits, but they often have serious consequences. Some police forces are so concerned at the number of accidents involving tailgating vehicles that they now video the offence and prosecute offenders.

Tailgating means that your view of the road ahead is seriously restricted and you're left with an impossible stopping distance.

If a vehicle in front brakes heavily you need time to react and move your foot to the brake pedal. At 50 mph you'll have travelled 15 metres (49 feet – more than the length of a coach) before you can start to brake. During that time the vehicle in front could have reduced its speed to below 40 mph.

Always maintain your safety margins. Considerate drivers also allow the driver following them ample time to react.

### Intimidation

Never use the size, weight and power of your vehicle to intimidate other road users. Even the repeated 'hiss' of air brakes being applied or released while stationary gives the impression of 'breathing down the neck' of the driver in front.

## Speed

You can never justify driving too fast just because you have to reach a given location by a specific time. Don't be tempted to drive faster when you've fallen behind schedule. If an accident happens and you injure someone there's no possible defence for your actions.

### Speed limiters

The introduction of speed limiters on coaches should have little effect on professional drivers. These devices merely prevent the vehicle exceeding the UK's maximum speed limit.

Not all coaches are required to have speed limiters. Those used before 1 April 1974 won't need them.

All coaches first used between 1 April 1974 and 31 December 1987 must have speed limiters fitted and set to no more than 112 kph (70 mph). Coaches used after 1 January 1988 must have them fitted and set to no more than 100 kph (62 mph). (Coaches are defined as PCVs over 7.5 tonnes with more than 16 seats.)

## Retaliation

You must resist the temptation to retaliate in order to 'teach someone a lesson'. Always drive

- Courteously
- With anticipation
- Calmly, allowing for other road users' mistakes
- In full control of your vehicle

You can't act hastily when driving a PCV without the possibility of serious loss of vehicle control.

### The horn

PCVs are often equipped with powerful horns and their use should be strictly confined to the guidance set out in *The Highway Code* – to warn other road users of your presence.

Never use the horn

- Aggressively
- Between 11.30 pm and 7 am in a built-up area
- When stationary, unless a moving vehicle poses a danger

### The headlights

There's only one official use of flashing the headlights described in *The Highway Code:* to let other road users know that you're there.

- Never repeatedly flash the headlights while driving directly behind another vehicle
- To avoid dazzle, don't put headlights on to full beam when following another vehicle
- Don't switch on auxiliary lights fitted to your vehicle unless weather conditions require them

### Misleading signals

Neither the horn nor the headlights should be used to rebuke or to intimidate another road user. By using unauthorised 'codes' of headlight or indicator flashing you may be misunderstood by others. This in turn could lead to accidents.

When driving abroad, headlamp flashing is used purely as a warning. Any other intention won't be understood.

## Effects of your vehicle

As a competent PCV driver you must always be aware of the effect your vehicle and your driving has on other road users.

You must recognise the effects of turbulence or buffeting your vehicle causes when overtaking

- Pedestrians
- Horse riders
- Cyclists
- Motorcyclists
- Cars
- Cars towing caravans
- Other buses and lorries

Smaller, lighter vehicles are also affected when they overtake you at speed, especially on motorways.

On congested roads, particularly in shopping areas, take extra care when you need to drive close to the kerb. Be aware of

- Pedestrians stepping off the kerb
- The danger of your nearside mirror striking the head of a pedestrian standing at the edge of the kerb
- Cyclists moving up on the nearside of your vehicle in slow-moving traffic

## Forces at work

You should understand something of the various forces that act on a vehicle and its passengers. The effects of these forces can seriously undermine your control so it's important to be aware of them and to act appropriately.

A basic law of physics states that a body will remain at rest or travel at a constant speed in a straight line unless acted upon by an external force. Therefore, a bus, coach or minibus travelling in a straight line under gentle acceleration is relatively stable.

When a vehicle

- Accelerates
- Brakes
- Changes direction

forces are applied to it and its load. The more violent or sudden the change, the greater the forces. Sudden, excessive or badly timed steering, braking and acceleration will introduce forces that can result in loss of control.

Steering should always be

- Smooth
- Planned
- Controlled
- Accurate

Braking should always be

- Progressive
- Correctly timed
- Smooth
- Sensitive

Acceleration should always be

- Progressive
- Used to best economic advantage
- Well planned
- Considerate

Most of the forces described in this book act on a vehicle in motion. If you disregard them you'll probably lose control, so allow for them in your driving.

### Friction

The resistance between two surfaces rubbing together is called friction. A tyre's grip on a road surface transmits 'traction', which is essential when

- Moving away or accelerating
- Turning/changing direction
- Braking/slowing down

The amount of grip will depend on

- The weight of the vehicle
- The vehicle's speed
- The condition of the tyre tread
- The tyre pressure
- The type and condition of the road surface
  - loose
  - smooth
  - anti-skid
- Weather conditions
- Any other material present on the road
  - mud
  - wet leaves
  - diesel spillage
  - other slippery spillages
  - inset metal rails
- Whether the vehicle's braking or steering sharply
- The condition of steering and suspension components

Sudden acceleration or braking can lead to loss of friction between the tyre tread and the road surface. Under these conditions the vehicle may

- Lose traction (wheelspin)
- Break away on a turn (skid)
- Not stop safely (skid)
- Overturn

The same will happen when changing into a lower gear if travelling too fast or if the clutch is suddenly released, because the braking effect will only be applied to the driven wheels.

## Inertia and momentum

A stationary bus with 70 or 80 passengers on board may weigh up to 18 tonnes. It requires a great deal of force to begin to move it, even on a flat road, but it takes relatively little power to keep it rolling at a constant speed. Resistance to change in a vehicle's state of motion is called inertia, and the force that keeps the vehicle rolling is called momentum.

Modern buses and coaches have engines with a high power output to

- Give good acceleration
- Overcome inertia

Passengers are also affected by these forces. A passenger's inertia has to be overcome in much the same way as the vehicle's. Acceleration will push them back into their seats, while braking will move their weight forward, due to momentum. Sudden braking will cause passengers to be thrown forward and could be dangerous. Therefore, all acceleration and braking should be as smooth, controlled and progressive as possible.

## Kinetic energy

The energy that's stored up in the vehicle and its passengers when travelling is known as kinetic energy. This is converted into heat at the brake shoes and drums when braking occurs.

Continuous use of the brakes results in them becoming over-heated and losing their effectiveness (especially on long downhill gradients). This effect is known as brake fade.

Much more effort is needed to stop a fully laden PCV than an ordinary car travelling at a similar speed. It's therefore important to avoid harsh braking. Plan ahead and take early action.

### Gravity

When a vehicle is stationary on level ground the only force acting upon it is the downward pull of gravity (ignoring wind forces, etc.). On an uphill gradient the effects of gravity will be much greater so that

- More engine power is needed to move the vehicle forward and upward
- Less braking effort is needed and the vehicle will pull up in a shorter distance

On a downhill gradient the effects of gravity will tend to

- Make the vehicle's speed increase
- Require more braking effort
- Increase stopping distances

The vehicle's centre of gravity is the point around which all its weight is balanced. All passenger vehicles are 'tilt tested' to ensure that the design is stable. But violent steering, acceleration or braking moves the centre of gravity and places excessive forces on the vehicle's tyres and suspension, and on the passengers.

Heavy braking whilst cornering can bring components very close to their design limits and will be uncomfortable for passengers. Catching a kerb or raised drain cover with a tyre under that sort of pressure could result in a blow-out and the vehicle going out of control or even overturning.

### Centrifugal force

When a vehicle takes a curved path at a bend the forces acting upon it tend to cause it to continue on the original, straight course. This is known as centrifugal force. At normal speeds this is overcome by the traction between the tyres and the road surface. However, if a bus or coach takes a bend too fast centrifugal force will cause the passengers to be thrown towards the outside of the bend.

## Maintaining control

You can't alter the severity of a bend or change the weight of the bus and its passengers. Similarly, you can't alter the design and performance characteristics of your vehicle and its components. But you **do** have control over the speed of your vehicle and the forces acting upon it.

If you ask too much of your tyres by turning and braking at the same time, you'll lose some of the available power and grip. When the tyres slide or lift you'll no longer be in full control of the vehicle. To keep control you should ensure that all braking is

- Controlled
- In good time
- Made when travelling in a straight line, wherever possible

Reduce speed and, where necessary, select the appropriate gear before negotiating

- Bends
- Roundabouts
- Corners

Avoid braking and turning at the same time, unless manoeuvring at low speed. Reduce your speed first and look well ahead to assess and plan.

## Vehicle sympathy

There are many different types of PCVs and each type requires different techniques to control it safely. Professional drivers will tell you that apparently identical buses each have a different 'feel'. They adapt their driving to suit the vehicle and develop what's known as 'vehicle sympathy'.

For example, drivers need to take corners slowly in order to keep their passengers comfortable. Yet it's difficult to define what 'slowly' means for all vehicles on all occasions. A safe, comfortable speed will depend on the sharpness of the corner and any other hazards there might be. The vehicle's design might dictate when the speed is comfortable.

New coaches have very sophisticated air-suspension levelling systems, which allow relatively fast cornering whilst maintaining the body almost level.

Information at the back of this book gives details on the type of licence needed to drive the different types of PCVs. This section discusses some of the basic characteristics of the various types of PCVs. However, it's up to you to develop your own 'vehicle sympathy' when driving.

## Minibuses

A minibus is generally defined as a small bus seating between nine and 16 passengers. They're often based on van bodies and have been adapted by specialist coach-building firms, although some manufacturers produce purpose-built vehicles. The controls are usually similar to those on cars.

Few minibuses are built for full public service use, where regulations require higher minimum standards for

- Headroom
- Access
- Seating
- Safety precautions
- Equipment
- Markings

### Driving minibuses

Driving a minibus is often a lot like driving a car. However, you need to be aware that despite power-assisted steering and braking, and possibly an automatic gearbox, they can be more demanding and tiring than driving a car.

You're strongly advised to seek professional training if you intend to drive minibuses. Various bodies run courses, but if you have difficulty finding one locally contact RoSPA, whose address and telephone number are at the back of this book.

Information at the back of this book tells you about licence requirements dependent on usage. Those vehicles operated under a community or minibus permit scheme are subject to special rules.

When driving a minibus you'll need to think about the

- Weight
  - greater stopping distances are needed
  - they're slower to accelerate and to overtake
  - more effort is needed for steering
- Height
  - there's greater body roll, pitch and sway
  - they're more susceptible to side winds, etc.
- Noise levels
  - these can be high, especially in van-derived models
  - passenger noise can be high and distracting
- Speeds
  - it's more difficult to maintain high average speeds
  - when fully laden, speed may be lost rapidly on uphill stretches of road
- Passengers comfort
- Distances travelled
  - is the vehicle suitable for long journeys?

  - would the use of a larger vehicle, possibly hired with a driver, be more appropriate?
- Time
  - plan your journey and estimate realistically how long it will take
  - allow plenty of time for the journey, thus putting yourself under less pressure
  - you'll need to take adequate breaks

Never drive for more than 4.5 hours without taking a break of at least 45 minutes. If you're subject to drivers' hours regulations you'll find that this rule, and others, are legal requirements.

Treat minibus driving as you would other work, even if it isn't your normal job. You need to be alert and to concentrate. Refer to the rules in Part Two, which apply to professional drivers, and consider the advice in the officially recommended syllabus in Part Four.

Ultimately, consider carefully before each journey whether

- You need someone else to drive
- A second driver is advisable

## Seat belts

Seat belts save lives and reduce the risk of injury. Current legislation requires **all** minibuses to be fitted with seat belts to **all** forward-facing seats when three or more children aged between 3 and 15 years (inclusive) are carried.

Minimum requirements are for a lap belt to be fitted to each seat occupied by a child. As a PCV driver you have a responsibility towards your passengers' safety, particularly when engaged in transporting children. All front-seat passengers are required to wear seat belts; rear-seat passengers should always wear belts if fitted.

If the minibus unladen weight (ULW) **is less than** 2,540kg it's the driver's responsibility to make sure that all rear-seat passengers aged between 3 and 15 years (inclusive) wear the appropriate seat belt or restraint.

- Children under 3 use an appropriate child restraint
- Children aged 3–11 and under 1.5 metres in height use an appropriate restraint or adult seat belt
- Children over 1.5 metres in height wear an adult seat belt

## Midibuses

There's no legal definition of a midibus. However, the term is generally used to describe any single-decker vehicle that's between a minibus and a 40+ seat coach or bus.

Virtually all are purpose-built and many have bus or coach controls, equipment and other systems. Some midibuses are specialist vehicles with wheelchair lifts and securing equipment. Many are used on normal services, where demand isn't sufficient to justify the use of full-size buses.

Seat belts save lives and reduce the risk of serious injury. All passengers should be encouraged to wear seat belts if they're fitted. School contract work is covered by specific legislation, which requires belts to be fitted and used.

Depending on the use and seating capacity, drivers require one of the following licence entitlements

- D
- D1
- D + E or D1 + E, if a trailer over 750kg is to be towed

Some midibuses operated under the community minibus and large bus permit schemes can be driven with a category B (car) licence. The rules are explained in booklet PSV 385, available from Traffic Area Offices.

It's essential that you fully understand the vehicle controls and, wherever possible, undergo 'type' training.

Many of the points relating to minibuses also apply to midibuses, as do many of the topics covered in the sections on buses and coaches. In particular, you'll need to consider

- Blind spots and restricted vision
- Standing passengers
- Careful use of automatic gearboxes, where fitted
- Body roll

## Single-decker service buses

These vehicles are generally designed for local bus service use and have basic passenger equipment. They may also have a limited amount of seating and a higher proportion of space for standing passengers. Most are one-person operated.

Newer vehicles are built to the Disabled Persons Transport Advisory Committee (DiPTAC) specification and may incorporate 'kneeling' suspension, wide doors and other design features to cater for customers with disabilities.

Because of the 'stop–start' nature of the journeys, most of these vehicles have semi-automatic or fully automatic gearboxes, although some buses with manual gearboxes are still in use. All have relatively low gearing, with only four or five gears, or are coupled to low-ratio drive axles to give greater flexibility at low speeds. As a result they may have lower top speeds.

Single-decker service buses require skill and sensitivity on the part of the driver if they're to be driven smoothly.

## Double-decker service buses

These are high-capacity vehicles used primarily for stage carriage work (refer to the Glossary of terms at the back of this book). Most are fitted with dual doors and fare-collection equipment to allow for effective one-person operation.

Additional internal mirrors are positioned to allow the driver to observe entrances, exits, stairs and the upper deck. To ensure high standards of passenger care and safety, drivers should make full use of them.

Automatic and semi-automatic gearboxes are frequently fitted to these vehicles. Make sure that you know how to make smooth gear changes and to use the gearbox correctly when moving off and pulling up. Vehicle manufacturers give advice for each type of vehicle.

Drivers need to balance safe driving techniques with the comfort of passengers and the need to keep to timetables. Smooth, skilful driving will be essential during peak periods when there will be more passengers standing, climbing the stairs and moving about the bus.

Most modern double-decker vehicles have underfloor or rear-mounted engines. You're less likely to know if the engine is overheating, for example, so you'll have to make full use of instruments and warning lights to ensure early action should a fault develop.

On double-decker buses the driving position and front entrance are generally ahead of the front axle whilst the position of rear axles varies considerably. The wheel-base of the bus will dictate the appropriate course to take when cornering. This means that you must take care with overhangs and be aware of the danger of tyre damage on kerbs, etc.

Read the information on vehicle height in Part Two and take extra care when driving open-top double-decker buses, such as 'sightseeing' tour buses and those operated in seaside towns.

## Articulated buses

Articulated buses consist of a two-axle lead unit coupled to a single-axle rear section by means of floor- and roof-level pivots and a flexible shroud. They offer high-capacity urban transport on routes where double-deckers are less practical.

Trials with articulated buses have taken place in a number of areas in the UK and their numbers are increasing. They're more common in other countries, particularly in Europe, where height limits of 4 metres (13 feet) exist. In this country their length – up to 18 metres long (59 feet) – can present problems when used on urban streets.

Additional care is needed when driving these vehicles. Always be aware of the 'swept path' the vehicle is taking. And remember, the rear section, unlike some large articulated goods vehicles, exactly 'tracks' the path taken by the lead section. 'Type' training is essential before driving an articulated bus.

When crossing road junctions and pulling into lay-bys allowances have to be made for the additional length of the vehicle. Don't obstruct other road users, and avoid getting into a situation that will require reversing the vehicle. Except if special video reversing equipment is fitted, don't attempt to reverse unless an assistant stands in view at the rear of the bus to help.

New drivers of vehicles towing trailers will need to take a category D + E test if the trailer is over a maximum authorised mass of 750kg. An articulated bus isn't deemed to be a bus towing a trailer and can therefore be driven on a category D licence.

Coach journeys are longer and frequently use motorways, so manual gearboxes remain the norm, but they often have six or more gears. Semi-automatic and fully automatic vehicles are in use and there's an increasing trend towards air suspension systems.

## Single-decker coaches

Coaches are designed to carry customers for longer distances, in greater comfort and with improved facilities. Many have sophisticated heating and air conditioning systems, toilets, catering areas and courier seats. Most modern vehicles are fitted with rear or underfloor engines to limit noise levels and so that more luggage can be carried.

If vehicles are fitted with video and television equipment it's illegal for their screens to be visible to the driver or the occupants of other vehicles. It's essential, therefore, that curtains are fitted and closed when this equipment is in use.

Special regulations apply to the charging, use, location and emptying of water and toilet systems fitted to road vehicles. See the relevant advice in the officially recommended syllabus in Part Four.

Coaches are often downgraded to dual-purpose or service-bus use after several years of operation. In addition, some rural bus operators use coaches so that their passengers travel in greater comfort. In such instances, lower specification running gear may be fitted to the vehicles to make it easier for the driver (less gear-changing, etc).

Seat belts save lives and reduce the risk of serious injury. Current legislation requires front seats level with, or forward of, the driver to have belts fitted if the coach was first used after 1 October 1988. School contract work or outings when three or more children between the ages of 3 and 15 years (inclusive) are carried require, as a minimum, a lap belt to be fitted to all forward-facing seats. Vehicles first used before 1 October 1988 will have to comply from 10 February 1998 if three or more children are carried.

## Double-decker coaches

The first double-decker coaches were introduced in the UK in the 1950s. They were based on bus body shells but were fitted with more powerful engines and higher gearing. Coach seats were added to provide high-capacity, luxury vehicles able to compete with other long-distance passenger transport.

Since then there have been considerable developments, not least in the facilities double-decker coaches now offer. Nearly all are now specially designed and purpose-built. Comfort and customer service are the biggest selling points. Although some double-decker coaches provide 70 or more seats, passenger-carrying capacity isn't always the key attraction to customers. These coaches may be fitted with

- Toilets
- Refreshment facilities
- Lounges
- Tables
- Telephones and fax machines
- Audio visual equipment
- Crew sleeping accommodation

A number of double-decker coaches have a courier service and some specialist vehicles are designed to carry as few as 12 passengers, with full sleeping or conference facilities provided.

The regulations governing video/ television equipment and waste water disposal are similar to those for single-decker coaches, and may be found in the syllabus in Part Four.

These coaches are amongst the most sophisticated vehicles on the road, with high-power units, versatile manual, automatic, semi-automatic or electronic gearboxes, air suspension and power-assisted controls. Make sure that you understand all the systems fitted to the vehicle and are fully competent to operate them.

Seat belt requirements are the same as for single-decker coaches.

Driving positions may be unusual in these vehicles, so

- The driver may not be able to see what's happening inside the coach
- Video or electronic sensor systems may be fitted to help with manoeuvring and to add to the view given by the rear view mirrors
- Additional mirrors may be fitted to show the driver what's happening below his field of vision at the front of the coach

Use all these aids when driving to help you to drive safely.

## Six-wheel double-deckers

Higher vehicle weight has meant that air suspension is being fitted increasingly to all but the lightest PCVs to counter the damaging effects on roads and bridges. Another recent development has been the addition of an extra rear axle to further distribute vehicle loads.

Although tri-axle coaches were popular in the 1930s before air suspension had been invented, few post-war vehicles were six-wheelers, except for some coaches in the 1960s when an extra steering axle was added to the front.

In fact, the new generation of three-axle buses and coaches may have eight or ten wheels – one or both of the rear axles carrying four road wheels.

Handling isn't greatly different from two-axle vehicles, except that punctures and blow-outs are sometimes difficult to detect. Frequent tyre checks are advised.

The course the wheels take on tight corners should be observed and allowed for when driving. Very low speed is advisable when the steering is on full lock to minimise any possible 'scrubbing' effect on the rearmost tyres.

Seat belts save lives and reduce the risk of serious injury. All passengers should be encouraged to wear seat belts if they're fitted. School contract work is covered by specific legislation, which requires belts to be fitted and used.

## Mobile project and playbuses

More than 500 double-and single-decker buses and coaches have been converted for community use in the UK. As their primary purpose is for recreational, vocational or educational use they aren't regarded as PCVs.

There are particular rules for their use and licensing requirements (see Part Six). They may, in some cases, be driven by category B (car) licence-holders. However, the driving requirements for these large vehicles are the same whether an additional driving test has to be taken or not. If you drive one of these vehicles it's essential that you're fully aware of your responsibilities.

This book tells you what's expected of professional PCV drivers, but the advice applies to anyone who drives buses or coaches. A book can teach you the basic facts and theory about driving, but you should always seek professional guidance before driving on public roads. You can't expect to drive a bus, whatever its present use, without adequate training.

Most mobile project and playbuses are elderly buses that are 'life expired' for PCV operations. The importance of safety checks and adequate maintenance is greater as a result. Drivers must be able to identify faults and understand procedures for putting them right.

Operators and drivers of mobile project and playbuses need to consider the safe

- Stowage of equipment when the bus is being driven
- Manoeuvring of the bus when arriving at, or departing from, sites
- Installation and stowage of any heating, lighting or cooking equipment, including gas cylinders
- Operation of generators and fuel storage

Detailed guidance is available from the National Playbus Association, whose address is at back of this book.

## Historic buses and coaches

Enthusiasts have ensured that many historic buses and coaches have been preserved and are shown at rallies.

Some of these historic vehicles may be driven on a category B (car) licence entitlement, provided certain rules are observed. These are

- The driver must be over 21
- The vehicle must carry less than eight passengers

Drivers with category D licence entitlements may drive historic buses and coaches as they would any other PCV.

You should seek professional training if you intend to drive historic buses and coaches. For example, you need to know how to 'double de-clutch' (refer to the Glossary of terms) or 'snatch-change' to use crash or part-synchromesh gearboxes. These are special techniques that you should practise after they've been explained and demonstrated to you. Also, if the vehicle you drive has air or vacuum brakes, make sure that you understand the meaning of any warning signals.

If you drive a historic vehicle for the first time start by mastering steering, gear-changing and braking techniques

- Off the road
- Under supervision
- Without passengers

Older buses and coaches are more difficult to drive than modern counterparts. Generally, there's no power steering, air-assisted clutches or semi-automatic gearboxes to make driving easier.

When driving these older vehicles

- Think how your slower speed affects other road users
- Pull over to let others pass, when you can do so safely
- Treat the vehicle with respect and ask for advice if you come across controls or warning systems that are unfamiliar
- Make sure that you have full control

It's important that you never drive a preserved vehicle unless you're certain that it's fully roadworthy. Carry out all the checks advised in Part Three and also make sure that you're competent to drive the vehicle.

## Passenger and general safety

Never drive a bus in which you have no contact with passengers without one designated, responsible person in charge of the passenger saloon(s). The exceptions to this are when no passengers are carried and when access to the vehicle is prevented by means of a door, chain, strap or other barrier. In addition, never

- Allow passengers to ride on open platforms or with open doors
- Allow more passengers to be carried than the vehicle is designed for, or the law allows
- Allow bells to be used other than in the accepted way. In half-cab vehicles this is the only means of communication between the passenger saloon(s) and the driver

Ensure that the bell codes are understood and that no one else uses the bell except to give the 'stop' signal, when necessary. The codes are

- One bell – stop when safe
- Two bells – move off when safe
- Three bells – bus full
- Four bells – emergency on bus

Always take great care on rally sites when pedestrians are close to moving vehicles. Drive only at walking pace, or slower, and use marshals or other responsible people to help you to manoeuvre safely.

## Light rail (or rapid) transit (LRT) systems

Trams are often referred to in several ways. They may be called light rapid transit (LRT) or 'metro' systems, or 'supertrams'. LRT systems are common throughout Europe and there are plans to introduce them to many more cities in the UK.

They're essentially modern tramways – the vehicles running singly or, more often, as multiple units on standard railway track gauge to light railway specifications. Some systems operate completely segregated from other traffic and may run on former railway tracks. LRT vehicles are fixed in the route they follow and can't manoeuvre around other vehicles and pedestrians.

The area occupied by an LRT vehicle is marked by paving or markings on the road surface. This 'swept path' must always be kept clear. Other road users, including bus and coach drivers, must avoid blocking 'supertram' routes.

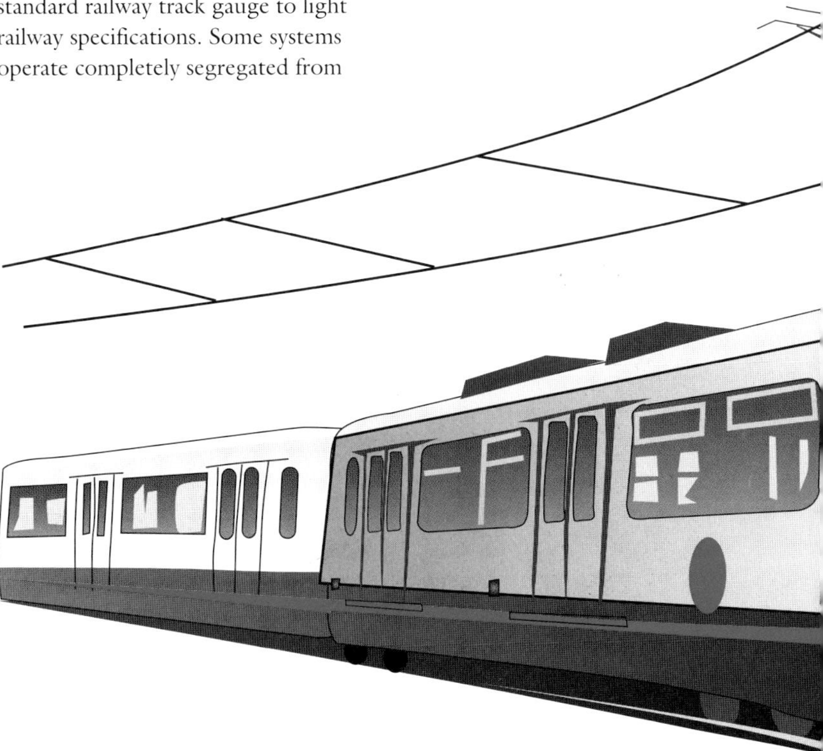

The following points are important

- In some towns and cities certain roads are restricted to buses and LRTs only
- Where LRTs operate on roads not segregated from other traffic, LRT drivers must hold full category B licence entitlement
- LRT drivers and vehicles are subject to all the normal rules of the road in addition to specific rules about LRT operation

Drivers are only permitted to operate 'supertrams' after extensive training. All UK LRT and traditional tram operators have dedicated training schools and staff to ensure high safety standards.

Other road users need to be aware of how to deal with LRTs – and of their limitations. When a tram approaches, other vehicles (and pedestrians) must

- Keep away from the swept path area
- Obey yellow box junction rules and not block junctions
- Anticipate well ahead and never stop on or across the tracks
- Obey all traffic light signals and never 'jump' lights that show the tram has priority

Open-top buses shouldn't be driven beneath overhead LRT power supply lines. Also, whenever possible, drivers of non-tram vehicles should avoid driving directly along metal rails, especially in wet weather, to avoid the risk of skidding.

## Tram signs

Warning of trams crossing ahead

Speed limit for tram drivers. (All diamond-shaped signs are only for tram drivers.)

Trams travel in both directions. All other traffic obeys one-way signs.

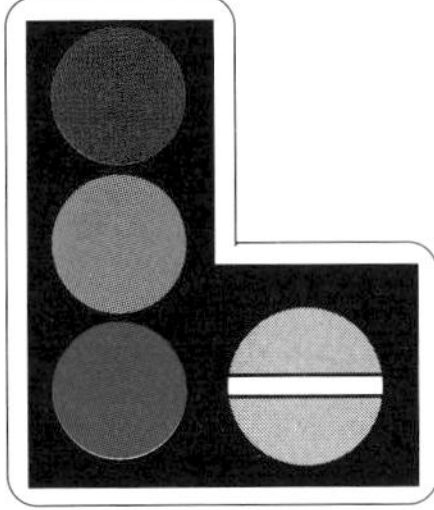

The signal mounted to the right gives instructions to tram drivers, which may not be the same as those given to drivers of other vehicles.

Reminder to pedestrians to look out for trams approaching from both directions

Lane for trams only

Route for trams only

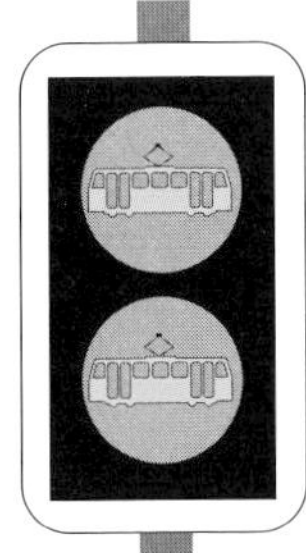

Warning signals for pedestrians. The lights flash when a tram is approaching.

## Towing trailers

Considerable care is needed when towing trailers, especially when reversing. Extensive training and practice are strongly recommended.

When you tow a trailer make sure that

- Access to emergency exits aren't obstructed
- You know and comply with the speed limits that apply to vehicles towing trailers
- You don't carry passengers in the trailer

New EC regulations are now in force covering the towing of trailers by motor vehicles. The information in Part Six details how this will affect drivers of PCVs.

## Braking systems

There are three braking systems fitted to PCVs.

### The service brake

- The principle braking system used
- Operated by the foot control
- Used to control the speed of the vehicle and to bring it to a halt safely
- May incorporate an anti-lock braking system (ABS)

### The secondary brake

- May be combined with the foot-brake control or the parking brake
- For use in the event of a failure of the service brake
- Normally operates on fewer wheels than the service brake and therefore has a reduced level of performance

### The parking brake

- Usually a hand control
- May also be the secondary brake but should normally only be used when the vehicle is stationary
- Must always be set when the vehicle is left unattended. (It's an offence to leave any vehicle without applying the parking brake.)

### Anti-lock braking systems (ABS)

Some vehicles are fitted with anti-lock braking systems (ABS). Wheel-speed sensors, featured in these systems, detect the moment during braking when a wheel is about to lock. Just before this happens the system reduces the braking effort and then rapidly re-applies it. This action may happen many times a second to maintain brake performance.

Preventing the wheels from locking means that the vehicle's steering and stability is also maintained, leading to safer stopping. But remember, an ABS is only a driver aid. It doesn't remove the need for good driving practices such as anticipating events and assessing road and weather conditions.

Anti-lock braking systems are commonly used on large PCVs and are required by law on some. It's important to ensure that an ABS is functioning before setting off on a journey. Driving with a defective ABS may constitute an offence.

The satisfactory operation of the ABS can be checked from a warning signal on the dashboard. The way the warning lamp operates varies between manufacturers, but with all types the light comes on with the ignition. It should go out no later than when the vehicle has reached a road speed of about 10 kph (6 mph).

### Endurance braking systems

Buses and coaches are also frequently equipped with endurance braking systems (commonly called retarders). These systems provide a way of controlling the vehicle's speed without using the wheel-mounted brakes.

Retarders operate by applying resistance, via the transmission, to the rotation of the vehicle's driven wheels. This may be achieved by

- Increased engine braking
- Exhaust braking
- Transmission-mounted electromagnetic or hydraulic devices

Endurance braking systems can be particularly useful on the descent of long hills, when the vehicle's speed can be stabilised without using the service brake. Braking generates heat so that, at high temperatures, braking performance can be reduced. Proper use of endurance braking systems can prevent this from happening.

The system may be operated with the service brake (integrated) or by using a separate hand control (independent). Retarders normally have several stages of effectiveness, depending on the braking requirement. With independent systems the driver has to select the level of performance required.

When operating independent retarders while driving on slippery roads care must be exercised if rear wheel locking is to be avoided. Some retarders are under the management of the ABS system to help avoid this problem.

## Safety

Air brake systems are fitted with warning devices that are activated when air pressure drops below a predetermined level. In some circumstances there may be sufficient pressure to release the parking brake even though the warning is showing. Under these circumstances the service brake may be ineffective. Therefore, you should never release the parking brake when the brake pressure warning device is operating.

On some vehicles a special brake may be automatically applied when the vehicle is brought to a stop. This is designed to prevent the vehicle moving until the accelerator is used to move off. This isn't a parking brake, however, so you shouldn't leave your seat until the parking brake has been applied.

## Inspection and maintenance

You aren't expected to be a mechanic, however there are braking system checks that **are** your responsibility, for example

**Air reservoirs** Air braking systems draw their air from the atmosphere, which contains moisture. This moisture condenses in the air reservoirs and can be transmitted around a vehicle's braking system. In cold weather this can lead to ice forming in valves and pipes and may result in air pressure loss and/or system failure. Some air systems have automatic drain valves to remove this moisture while others require daily manual draining. You should establish whether your vehicle's system reservoirs require manual draining and, if so, whose responsibility it is to make sure it's done.

**Controls** Before each journey make sure that all warning systems are working. Brake pressure warning devices can be activated by using a special 'check' switch. If an ABS is fitted this should be done only when the ABS warning light is operating. In any case, the ignition should be switched on first. Never start a journey with a defective warning device or when the warning is showing.

If the warning operates when you're travelling, stop as soon as you can do so safely and seek expert assistance. Driving with a warning device operating may be very dangerous and is an offence.

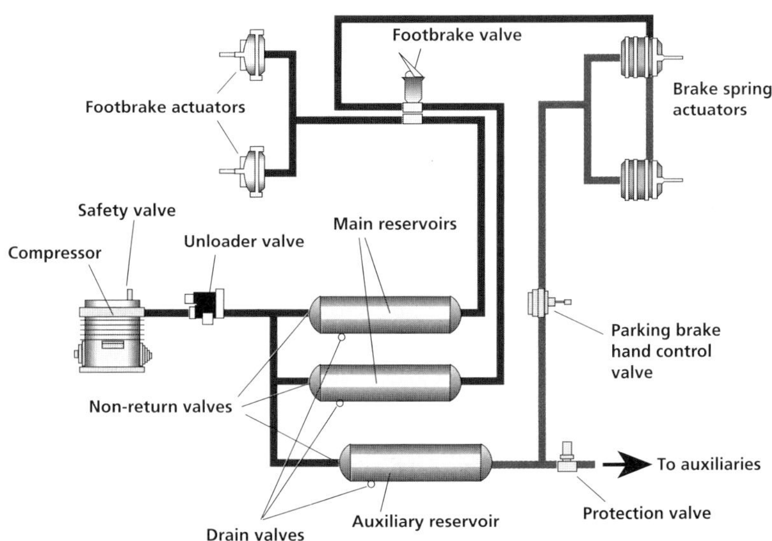

### Auxiliary air systems

Modern PCVs may be equipped with air-operated accelerators, clutches, gear-change mechanisms, wipers, doors, suspension, ramps, lifts or 'kneeling' devices. Operation of these may influence the vehicle's braking systems.

Drivers should familiarise themselves with the function and effect of these systems and be aware of any 'interlinks' that may be fitted. For example, air-operated accelerators may be disabled when the passenger doors are open, etc.

### Power-assisted steering (PAS)

Older and smaller vehicles often rely on the driver's own effort when turning the steering wheel to steer the vehicle's front wheels. So that this effort is reasonable, a gearing system is used. The driver may need to turn the steering wheel several times to reach 'full lock' (the tightest turn the vehicle can make). With historic buses it's necessary to drive more slowly round corners in order to give yourself enough time to turn the wheel.

To reduce the effort required and the amount that the driver has to turn the steering wheel, many modern minibuses, buses and coaches are fitted with a power-assisted system (PAS). This uses an engine-driven pump to supply hydraulic fluid under pressure, which operates 'rams' attached to the steering arms.

PAS reduces the driver's efforts when turning. However, it only operates when the engine is running. If a fault develops you can retain control of the steering, but much greater effort is needed to turn the steering wheel. Movement at the steering wheel may also be felt as a series of jerks.

Don't attempt to drive a vehicle fitted with PAS

- Without the engine running, that is, 'coasting'
- If the system is faulty

If a fault develops whilst travelling, stop as soon as you can safely do so and seek expert assistance.

# PART TWO LIMITS AND REGULATIONS

This part looks in detail at the limits, rules and regulations that you'll need to know and follow when you become a professional PCV driver.

## The topics covered

- Vehicle limits
- Environmental impact
- Legal requirements
- Other regulations

## Basic knowledge

The passenger transport industry is subject to a wide range of regulations and requirements relating to

- Drivers
- Operators
- Companies
- Vehicles
- Passengers
- Workshops

The first thing you'll need to know about is your vehicle. The various aspects to consider are its

- Weight (restrictions)
- Height (clearances, etc.)
- Width (restrictions)
- Length (lay-bys, corners)
- Ground clearance (for humpback bridges, grass verges, kerbs, etc.)

You'll also need to know the various speed limits that apply to your vehicle and the speeds at which it will normally travel and cruise.

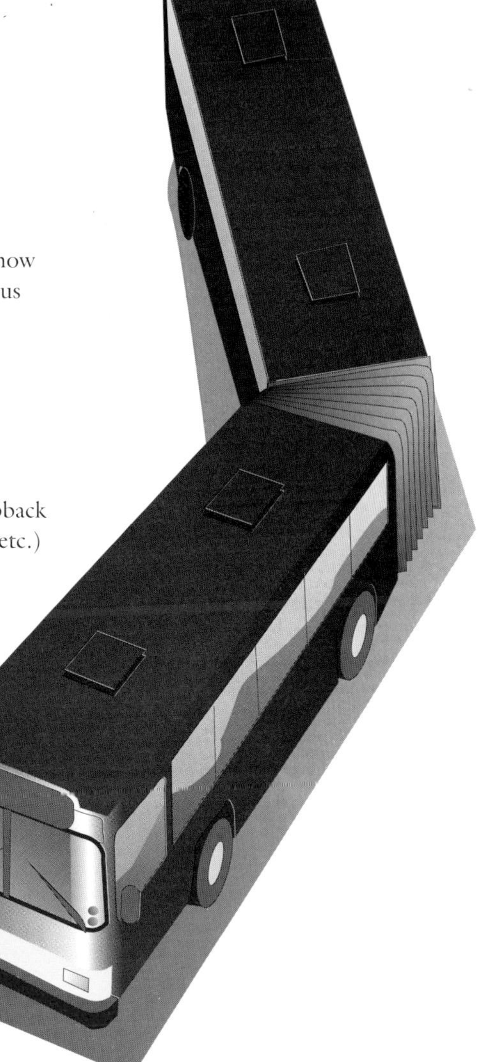

## Weight

Weight limits are imposed on roads and bridges for two reasons

- The structure may not be capable of carrying greater loads
- To divert larger vehicles to more suitable routes

Sometimes buses and coaches are exempt from the notified limits by means of a plate beneath the weight limit sign. This normally refers to PCVs in service or requiring to use that particular road for access. If you can use another route, do so. Remember, try to be considerate towards local people and the environment.

You should be aware of, and understand, the limits relating to any vehicle you drive. Certainly you should make sure that you know what your vehicle weighs.

In many cases, weight limits apply to the maximum gross weight (MGW). To arrive at this figure add about 1 tonne per 15 passengers to the unladen weight shown on your vehicle plus an allowance for any luggage you may be carrying. For example

| | |
|---|---|
| 75-seat double-decker coach | 12.0 tonnes |
| 75 passengers | 5.0 tonnes |
| 75 cases | 1.5 tonnes |
| 500 litres fuel | 0.5 tonnes |
| **Total weight** | **19.0 tonnes** |

The weight difference between a laden and unladen coach may be as much as 7 tonnes.

Definitions of terms to do with weight limits can be found in the Glossary of terms at the back of this book.

## Height

You aren't allowed to drive a vehicle that has an overall travelling height of more than 3.66 metres (12 feet) unless the overall travelling height (including any trailer) is conspicuously marked

- In feet and inches, or in feet and inches and in metres so that there's no more than 50 mm difference between the height specified in feet and inches and the height specified in metres
- In figures at least 40 mm high, which can be read by the driver when in the driving position

In addition, you should ensure that

- Any height indicated isn't less than the overall travelling height of the vehicle
- This is the only indication of the overall travelling height

### Overhead clearances

Drivers of any vehicle exceeding 3.66 metres (12 feet) in height should exercise care when entering

- Loading bays
- Bus and coach stations
- Depots
- Refuelling areas
- Service station forecourts
- Any premises that have overhanging canopies

or when driving under or negotiating

- Bridges
- Overhead cables
- Overhead pipelines
- Overhead walkways
- Road tunnels

The normal maximum permitted overall travelling height of any PCV with fixed bodywork is 4.57 metres (15 feet). Many countries in the EC don't allow PCVs in excess of 4 metres (13 feet) without an exceptional vehicle permit being applied for, and issued, in advance.

Be aware of overhanging tree branches, particularly on roads rarely used by high vehicles, in case upper-deck windows are broken. Trees on regularly used routes are generally kept trimmed. If in doubt, slow right down and, if necessary, stop, get out and check.

### Don't take chances.

In addition, most roads have a slope (camber) to help with drainage, however this can sometimes cause problems. For example, on roads with a severe camber the top of a double-decker bus can lean up to 250 mm (around 10 in.) further over than the wheels. This situation could be made worse when pulling up at bus stops, if the nearside wheels drop into the gutter. Lamp-posts, traffic signs, shop awnings, bus shelters, etc. are within this 'danger zone', so watch out for these hazards.

## Bridges

Every year there are about 750 accidents where vehicles hit railway or motorway bridges, some involving buses and coaches. This means that, on average, there are **more than two incidents every day of the year**.

Collisions involving buses can kill or injure passengers, not to mention weaken the bridge. When a railway bridge is involved, such a collision frequently disrupts rail traffic and could lead to a major disaster. There are also the additional costs involved in making the bridge safe, re-aligning railway tracks, etc., apart from the general disruption to road and rail traffic.

The headroom under bridges in the UK is at least 5 metres (16 feet 6 in.), unless otherwise indicated. Where the overhead clearance is arched this is normally **only** between the limits marked.

You **must** know the height of your vehicle: don't guess. If in doubt, measure it or look at the information shown in the cab.

Don't ignore height restrictions shown on

- Traffic signs
- Road markings
- Warning lights

Stay alert to the dangers.

**Don't take chances.**

Railtrack 24-hour bridge hotline
0345 003 355

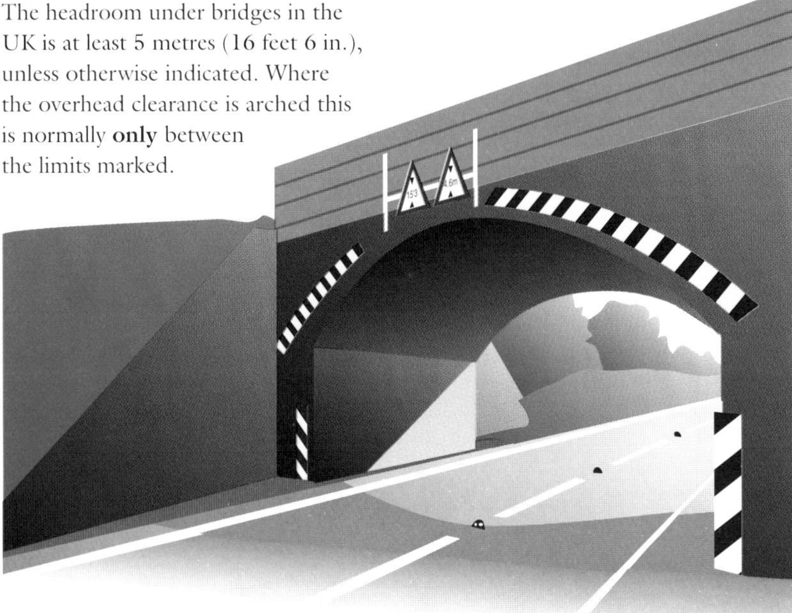

If your vehicle collides with any bridge **STOP**. Your first responsibility is to your passengers so check that there are no injuries. If there are, take appropriate action (see the advice on First Aid in Part Three).

If a railway bridge is involved you must report the incident to the police and to Railtrack at the time or, in any case, to the police within 24 hours. Failure to do so is an offence.

Never be tempted to 'hit and run': the consequences are unthinkable. To avoid a possible serious accident and loss of life report any incident immediately. Give information about

- The location
- The damage
- Any bridge reference number (often found painted on the bridge support or on a plate bolted to the bridge or wall)

If you aren't not sure of the safe height of a railway bridge stop and call Railtrack. To avoid problems

- Plan your route carefully
- Slow down when approaching bridges
- Know the height of your vehicle
- Keep to the centre of arched bridges
- Wait for a safe gap to proceed if there's oncoming traffic

## Height guide

| Metres | Feet/Inches |
|---|---|
| 5.0 | 16 6 |
| 4.8 | 16 |
| 4.5 | 15 |
| 4.2 | 14 |
| 3.9 | 13 |
| 3.6 | 12 |
| 3.3 | 11 |
| 3.0 | 10 |
| 2.7 | 9 |

## Width

You must always be aware of the road space your vehicle occupies. This is particularly important where road width is restricted because of parked or oncoming vehicles, or in narrow roads.

Many local authorities now use 'traffic calming' measures, which often include road width restrictions. Watch out for these. If you know of roads with such restrictions try to avoid them, unless you're following a scheduled service route, of course.

The majority of buses and coaches in the UK are 2.5 metres wide (8 feet 3 in.) but width can vary slightly between different makes. Mirrors and exterior trim can also add to a vehicle's width.

Where space is limited, take particular care when meeting other large vehicles. If necessary, stop first and, only if you're certain there's enough space, manoeuvre past slowly. Keep a lookout all round and especially watch out for mirrors hitting each other or lamp-posts, etc. A broken mirror means that your vehicle is unroadworthy and, therefore, illegal. It could also cause injury to you or others.

## Length

You need to know the length of your vehicle, as well as its width, so that you can judge the space you need on the road. You'll also need to know these dimensions to comply with regulations that affect your vehicle.

Other than 'traffic calmed' zones, places where there are restrictions on vehicle length are comparatively rare. Examples are

- Road tunnels
- Level crossings
- Ferries

The usual maximum length for a bus or coach is 12 metres (39 feet 4 in.). Articulated buses may be up to 18 metres long (59 feet), although these require special dispensation.

Drivers of long vehicles must be careful when

- Turning left or right
- Negotiating roundabouts or mini-roundabouts
- Emerging from premises or exits
- Overtaking
- Parking, especially in lay-bys
- Driving on narrow roads where there are passing places
- Negotiating level crossings

Be aware of the amount of space you need to turn (the 'turning circle') and the way that your vehicle overhangs kerbs and verges (the 'swept area').

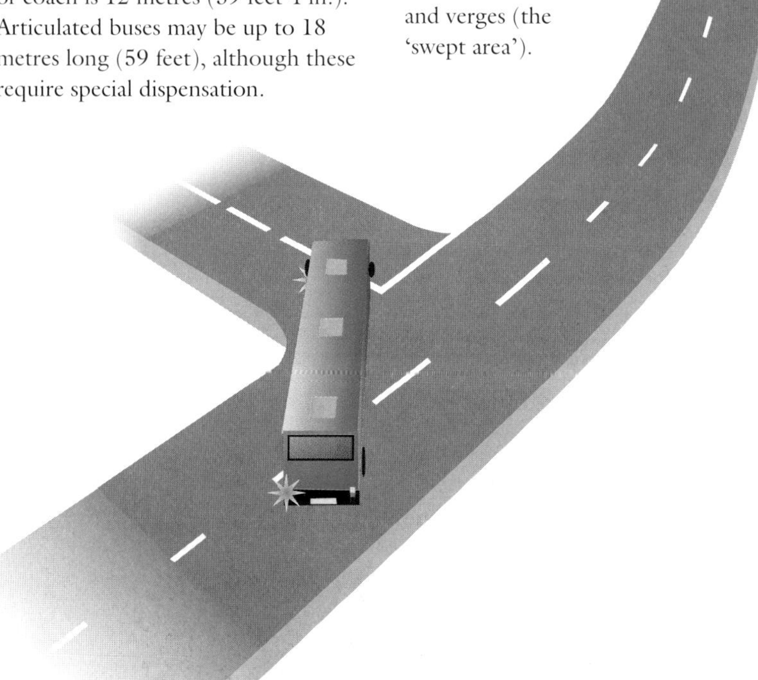

## Environmental issues

Vehicle designers, bus operators and maintenance staff all have a part in helping to reduce the effects that vehicles have on the environment. You can also help. You should be aware of the effects your vehicle, and the way in which it's driven and operated, can have on the environment around you.

The bus and coach industry has a major role to play in limiting the total number of vehicles on our roads. One double-decker bus can carry the occupants of 20 cars. Therefore, only one engine could be running instead of 20. And yet a badly maintained or poorly driven bus can cause unnecessary pollution, perhaps as much as several cars.

Make regular checks of your vehicle and ensure that any defects are reported and sorted out, especially

- Excessive exhaust smoke (the public is encouraged to report vehicles emitting excessive fumes)
- Uneven running, which may be caused by fuel pump or injector faults
- Brake faults, which can cause drag
- Incorrect tyre pressures
- Suspension system faults, which may result in road damage

Always drive with fuel economy in mind. Operators keep careful checks on vehicle running costs, and fuel economy is a key factor for profitability as well as reducing waste.

- Plan routes to avoid congestion
- Anticipate well ahead
- Avoid the need to 'make up time'
- Avoid over-revving (If a rev counter is fitted try to keep in the green band as much as possible.)
- Brake in good time (all braking wastes energy in the form of heat)
- Where regenerative retarders are fitted make good use of them
- Switch off your engine when stationary for some time, especially where noise and exhaust fumes cause annoyance
- Allow air pressure to build up with the engine on 'tick over' rather than 'revving up'

## Road-friendly suspension

Bumping your vehicle over kerbs, verges and pavements damages them and can also affect underground services. Repairs can be costly. Many PCVs are fitted with air suspension to reduce wear on road surfaces.

Damage to your vehicle's tyres, which may not be immediately obvious, can also be the result of poor driving and bad suspension. Subsequent tyre failure may have serious consequences, possibly to another driver and his or her passengers. Make sure that you drive responsibly and with due care, even if your vehicle isn't fitted with road-friendly suspension.

## Fuels

Take care to avoid spillages when you refuel your vehicle. Diesel fuel is slippery and can be very dangerous if stepped on (especially in garage areas). On the road it can create a serious risk to other road users, especially motorcyclists. It's a legal requirement that you check all filler caps are properly closed and secure before driving off.

PCV engines usually run on diesel fuel but a number of alternative fuels are becoming available.

### Compressed Natural Gas (CNG)

Although the quality of exhaust emissions produced has improved, there are technical problems with the size and design of the required tanks.

### Methane and Hydrogen

Experiments are being carried out to assess whether these naturally occurring fuels could be used as alternatives to diesel.

### Electricity

Trials have been taking place with electric vehicles for a number of years, but it's only recently that developments in overcoming the problems of battery size and capacity have occurred.

## Audible warning systems

Some vehicles are fitted with systems which warn people that the vehicle is reversing, such as

- Bleepers
- Horns
- Voice warnings

These must not be allowed to operate on a road subject to a 30 mph speed limit between 11.30 pm and 7 am. And remember, using an audible warning device doesn't take away the need to practise good, all-round effective observation.

Also, take care when setting vehicle alarm systems. There are restrictions on the length of time that the warning may sound. Environmental Health officers are empowered to enter vehicles and disable the system if a nuisance is caused.

There's a huge amount of legislation that affects the bus and coach driver. However, it's not within the scope of this book to explain fully all the rules that apply. This section outlines how to comply with EC and UK drivers' hours and tachograph rules.

## Tachographs

Tachographs are needed under EC rules

- For all vehicles with more than 16 passenger seats, except for those on regular services or those which are otherwise exempt
- For all vehicles with more than 8 passenger seats on EC international journeys

There are regulations that require tachographs to be

- Correctly calibrated before first use
- Inspected every two years
- Recalibrated after six-years' use

### Charts

Although there are exceptions, the basic requirements are that

- The driver must carry enough charts of an approved type, which can be used in the instrument fitted to the vehicle, for the whole journey
- Dirty or damaged charts must not be used

### Recording information

The driver must fill in all the information detailed in the centre field of each chart before use.

You must record all periods of work on the chart, ensuring the correct setting of the 'mode' switch at all times. This switch shows when the driver is

- Driving
- Carrying out other work
- Resting or taking a break

If you're working away from the vehicle and can't leave a chart in the tachograph – or have left the chart in but you've changed your work mode while away from the vehicle – you must make a manual entry on the reverse of the chart to that effect.

### Chart inspection

Drivers must carry their record charts for the current week and the last day of the previous week on which they drove. Completed charts must be given to employers within 21 days. Employers must make regular checks to ensure that the rules are being obeyed. The charts must be kept for at least one year after their use and submitted to enforcement authorities as required.

## EC drivers' hours

### Daily driving

You may drive for a maximum of nine hours a day (which may be increased to ten hours twice a week).

### Daily rest periods

After 4.5 hours of cumulative or continuous driving, a break of 45 minutes must be taken. This may be replaced by other breaks of at least 15 minutes each, which occur either during, or during and after, the 4.5 hours' driving period. However, this is provided they add up to at least 45 minutes in the 4.5 hours' driving period. It's generally accepted that a new driving period begins after 45 minutes' total break time has been taken.

### Weekly driving

Drivers aren't allowed to drive for more than six days in any one week and must not drive for more than 90 hours in any one fortnight.

### Weekly rest periods

You're also required to take a weekly rest period, which normally comes to 45 consecutive hours.

### Catching up on reduced rest

Minimum daily rest is 11 hours, although this may be reduced to nine hours on three days of the week. This is provided the reduction is compensated for by an equivalent rest period before the end of the week. Alternatively, 12 hours' daily rest may be taken in two or three periods, the last of which must be at least eight consecutive hours (and all of which must be of at least one hour).

### Two or more drivers

The rules on daily rest are different for vehicles staffed by two or more drivers, and for drivers of vehicles that cover part of their journey by ferryboat or train.

### Regular services

A regular service on a route of over 50 km is subject to EC rules, but a tachograph isn't needed as long as

- The employer draws up a service timetable and duty roster for crew members, records of which are kept for inspection
- The driver carries an extract from the duty roster and a copy of the service timetable

A regular service on a route of up to 50 km is free from the EC rules but will, in most cases, be subject to other rules.

Vehicles operating services under the 'permit' scheme may not require tachographs or be subject to the EC rules. The requirements will be explained when the permit is issued and will depend on the use made of the vehicle.

## Domestic drivers' hours

The domestic rules apply to those vehicles on journeys within the UK that are specifically exempted from the EC rules. No records are required for drivers of PCVs.

### Daily driving

You may drive ten hours on any working day (including any driving carried out under EC or AETR rules).

The length of the working day should be no more than 16 hours between starting and finishing work (including work other than driving and off-duty periods during the working day).

### Daily rest periods

You're allowed to drive continuously or cumulatively up to 5.5 hours. After this a break of at least 30 minutes must be taken for rest and refreshments. Alternatively, within any period of 8.5 hours in the working day, total breaks of at least 45 minutes should be taken so that you don't drive for more than seven hours 45 minutes. You must also have a break for rest or refreshment of at least 30 minutes at the end of this period, unless it's the end of the working day.

Ten hours' continuous rest must be taken between two working days. This can be reduced to 8.5 hours up to three times a week.

### Fortnightly rest periods

In any two weeks in a row (Monday to Sunday) there must be at least one period of 24 hours off duty.

### Exemptions

Those drivers who don't drive for more than four hours a day in any week are free from domestic rules for that week.

If you drive for more than four hours for up to two days in any week you're still free from the rules, but on each of these two days

- All working duties must start and finish within a 24-hour period
- You must have ten hours' rest in a row, immediately before the first duty and immediately after the last duty
- The rules on driving times and length of working day must be obeyed

If any working day overlaps into a week in which the driver isn't exempt from the rules, then on that day the driver must obey the limits on driving time and length of working day.

Any time spent dealing with an emergency will release the driver from the rules on driving time and rest periods.

## Mixed EC and domestic rules

You may find yourself working partly under EC rules and partly under UK domestic rules (sometimes even on the same day). In situations where you work 'mixed' hours you must know which set of rules to apply.

- Driving symbol

- Other work symbol

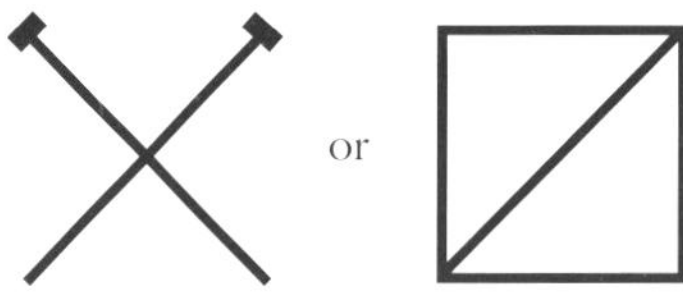

- On duty and available for work

- Break or rest symbol

Remember the following points

- When driving under each set of rules you must comply with the requirements of the specific rules being followed
- Time spent driving or on duty under one set of rules can't count as a break or rest period under the other set of rules
- Driving and other duties under EC rules count towards the limits on driving and other duties under UK domestic rules
- Driving and other duties under UK domestic rules (including non-driving work in other employment) count as 'attendance at work' under EC rules

### Recording 'mixed' hours

Tachographs aren't required under UK domestic rules but you'll need to make a manual entry on your tachograph chart, showing periods of domestic driving as 'other work', when driving under EC rules.

If you're using a tachograph when driving under domestic rules the mode switch should be set on 'other work'.

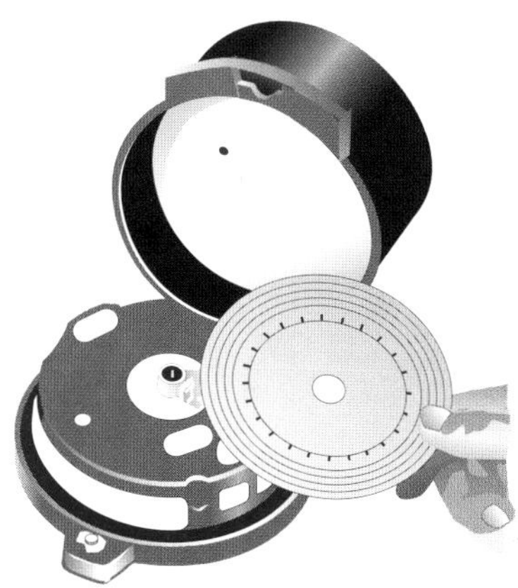

## Know the regulations

The number of people killed or injured on UK roads is a constant cause for concern. Better driver education and vehicle design, and tougher legislation, have helped to improve driving standards and to outlaw unsafe practices.

The laws covering PCVs and their drivers are extensive and sometimes complex, but their introduction has helped to give the industry a justifiably good safety record. And yet there are still about 10,000 casualties in accidents involving buses and coaches every year. Most of the injuries sustained aren't serious, but each year some 30 passengers are killed.

There's an average of more than 30 incidents involving PCVs every day. A small, but significant, proportion of those incidents involve a PCV driver breaking the law in some way. Drivers are also prosecuted for offences where no accident has occurred. Don't let this happen to you.

You must comply with regulations that affect

- Your health and conduct
- Your vehicle
- Your driving
- Your passengers
- Health and Safety issues

Remember, ignorance isn't accepted as a defence in law – even though the regulations concerned might only have changed the day before.

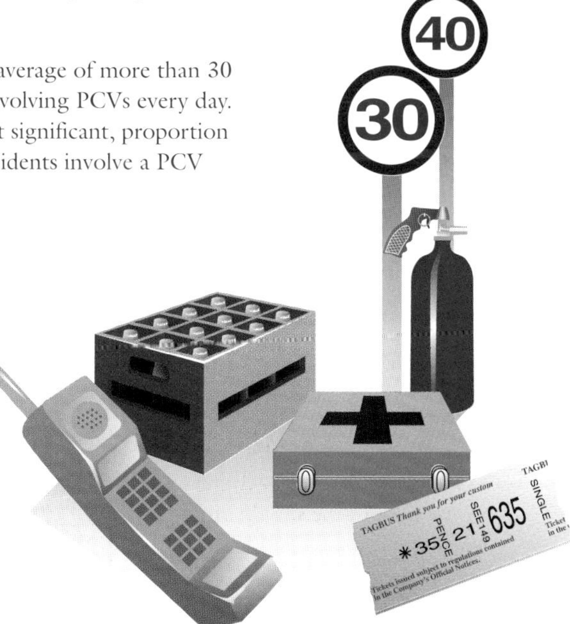

## Your health and conduct

### Health

Even apparently simple illnesses can affect your reactions. You should be on your guard against the effects of

- A common cold
- Flu symptoms
- Hay fever
- Tiredness

### Falling asleep

Previously unexplained incidents, where vehicles have

- Left the road
- Collided with broken-down vehicles, police patrol officers or other people on the hard shoulders of motorways

have now been attributed to the problem of drivers falling asleep at the wheel.

When driving you may feel tired for reasons that you may not appreciate. Be on your guard against boredom on comparatively empty roads or motorways, especially at night. Always

- Take planned rest breaks
- Keep a plentiful supply of fresh air circulating around the driving area
- Avoid allowing the driving area to become too warm
- Avoid driving if you aren't 100% fit
- Avoid driving after a heavy meal

Being a professional means making sure that you're fit for work. That includes making sure that you get enough rest the night before an early start. You have to be capable of driving safely for the whole of your shift. If you do start to feel tired or unable to concentrate, stop as soon as it's safe and legal to do so.

You may have to call out a relief driver if you're unable to continue or you're ill. It's much better to seek help rather than try to 'push on'. Try not to worry about inconveniencing your passengers or the company. It's better to arrive late than not at all.

Modern vehicles with air suspension, power steering and automatic transmission demand less of drivers than used to be the case. However, modern road and traffic conditions continue to demand just as much concentration as ever. Most accidents occur as a result of a lapse in concentration. Don't let one happen to you.

## Alcohol

It's an offence to drive with

- A breath alcohol level in excess of 35 microgrammes per 100 ml
- A blood alcohol level in excess of 80 mg per 100 ml

Alcohol may remain in the body's system for around 24 hours. So, you could still fail a breath test the morning after drinking. The only safe limit, ever, is a zero limit.

**Don't drink if you're going to drive.**

If you're convicted of a drink-driving offence while driving a car, any subsequent driving ban will mean that you also lose your PCV entitlement. That could mean losing your job. It's not worth the risk.

## Drugs

Some operators, concerned about drug abuse amongst staff, have introduced random drug-testing for their drivers. Drivers who fail such tests face instant dismissal.

You must not take any of the following drugs, classified as 'banned substances', whilst driving

- Amphetamines (e.g., 'diet pills')
- Barbiturates (sleeping pills)
- Benzodiazapine (tranquillizers)
- Cannabis
- Cocaine
- Heroin
- Methaqualone (sleeping pills)
- Methylamphetamines (MDMA)
- Morphine/codeine
- Phencyclidine ('Angel Dust')
- Propoxyphane

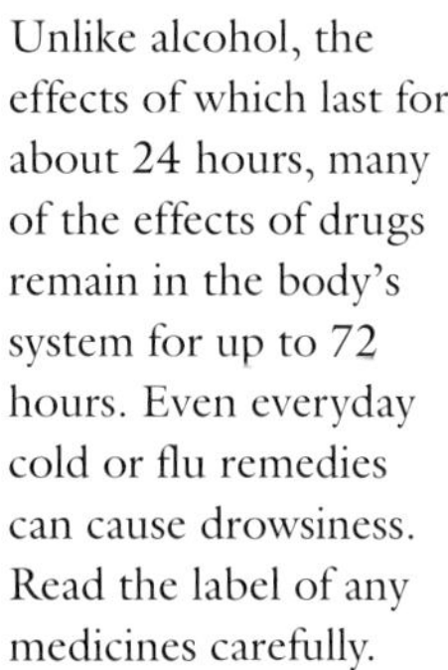

Unlike alcohol, the effects of which last for about 24 hours, many of the effects of drugs remain in the body's system for up to 72 hours. Even everyday cold or flu remedies can cause drowsiness. Read the label of any medicines carefully.

If in doubt, consult either your doctor or pharmacist. If still in doubt, **don't drive.**

## Your vehicle

The law relating to vehicles is extensive. Manufacturers, operators and drivers all must obey specific regulations.

The manufacturer is responsible for ensuring that the vehicle is built to comply with the Construction and Use Regulations.

The operator is responsible for making sure that a vehicle

- Continues to comply with those regulations
- Meets all current requirements and new regulations as they're introduced
- Is tested as required
- Displays all required markings, discs and certificates
- Is in a serviceable condition, including equipment, fittings and fixtures

In addition, the operator must operate a system whereby drivers of the vehicle can report defects and have them solved effectively. The operator shouldn't cause or permit a vehicle to be operated in any way other than the law allows.

The driver is responsible for

- Taking all reasonable precautions to ensure that legal requirements are met before driving any vehicle
- Checking that the vehicle is fully roadworthy and free from significant defects before driving it
- Ensuring that any equipment, fittings or fixtures required are present and serviceable
- Not driving the vehicle if any fault develops that would make it illegal to be driven
- Ensuring that all actions taken whilst in charge of the vehicle are lawful

You should consider whether it would be illegal to drive the vehicle if anything that should by law be fitted to or carried on the vehicle isn't in place or in a serviceable condition.

Similarly, if something is fitted to the vehicle which isn't required by law but is

- Unserviceable
- In a dangerous condition
- Not fitted so as to comply with the regulations

you should consider its legal status. For example, your vehicle isn't required by law to have spot or fog lights. However, if they're fitted they must be positioned according to the regulations. It's also an offence if they don't work.

## Speed limiters

EC legislation requires that buses and coaches over 7.5 tonnes gross vehicle weight and capable of speeds over 100 kph (62 mph) must be fitted with a speed limiter set to 100 kph if first used on or after 1 January 1988 on

- National journeys
- International journeys

The speed at which the limiter is set must be shown on a plate displayed in a conspicuous position in the driver's cab.

As a result of the fitting of speed limiters set to 100 kph (62 mph), buses and coaches may not use the right-hand lane(s) on motorways with more than two lanes for an initial two-year trial period from 1 January 1996.

## Your driving

When driving, it's your responsibility to follow all the relevant regulations. You must keep up to date with the road traffic rules and apply them.

This book covers the approach that you should take as a professional PCV driver. It doesn't include general driving principles – that is, everything that you should know and apply when driving **any** vehicle.

You may wish to refer to other books in the DSA Driving Skills series, such as *The Driving Test* and *The Driving Manual*. You should also refer to *The Highway Code* to keep up to date with revisions in traffic rules and any new road signs that may be introduced. Books by other publishers also cover general driving rules and regulations.

Keep in mind that ignorance of the law is no defence. It's reasonable to expect that you, as a professional driver, will be knowledgeable.

### Your driving licence

You need your PCV licence in order to earn your living driving buses, coaches and minibuses. To keep it you'll want to drive to a high professional standard.

When you drive any other vehicle – your own car, for example – it's essential that your driving continues to be to the same high standard.

Your PCV licence will be at risk if you accumulate penalty points from offences committed whilst driving **any** vehicle.

### Speeding offences

Many police forces and local authorities now use up-to-date technology to persuade drivers to obey speed limits, and to catch and prosecute those who don't.

Sophisticated detection equipment can 'lock on' to individual vehicles in busy traffic flows. Cameras can photograph vehicles exceeding the speed limit. At some motorway sites, roadside detection equipment displays the registration number and speed of vehicles to 'show up' the drivers concerned.

Speeding drivers who've been prosecuted find that the penalties are often linked to how much the legal speed limit was exceeded. But remember, the aim is to improve driving standards, not to increase prosecutions.

Your vehicle will probably be fitted with a speed limiter, which will generally prevent you from exceeding motorway speed limits. However, it won't stop you exceeding lower speed limits. Observing speed limits is part of your responsibility.

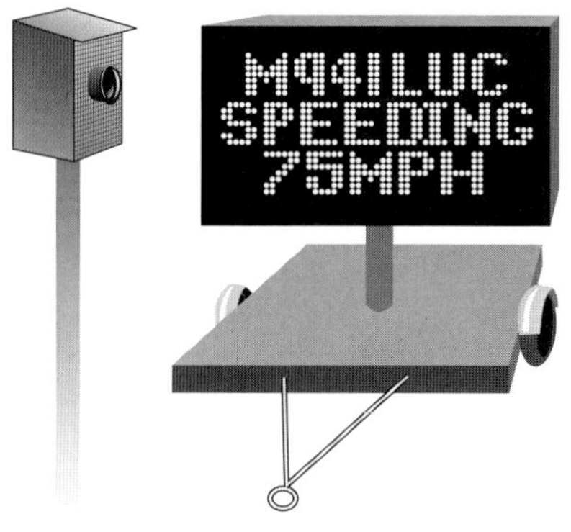


Any photograph produced as evidence and that shows the

- Time
- Date
- Speed
- Vehicle registration number
- Length of time a red signal had been showing

will prove difficult to dispute.

### Red light cameras

Cameras are increasingly being installed at light-controlled junctions to record drivers who don't comply with the signals. These cameras are also intended to act as a deterrent and to improve safety in general for road users.

## Red Routes

On many roads in London yellow lines are being replaced with red lines. A network of priority (Red) routes for London was approved by Parliament in June 1992 as a means of addressing traffic congestion problems and widespread disregard of parking restrictions in the capital. Work is now under way to introduce Red Route measures on 315 miles of London's most important roads by the year 2000. On these roads new Red Route signs and red markings are being introduced to replace the old yellow-line restrictions.

Yellow-line exemptions **don't** apply on Red Routes. During the day loading is only allowed in marked boxes. Overnight and on Sundays most controls are relaxed to allow unrestricted stopping. It's important to check signs carefully as the hours of operation for Red Routes vary from area to area.

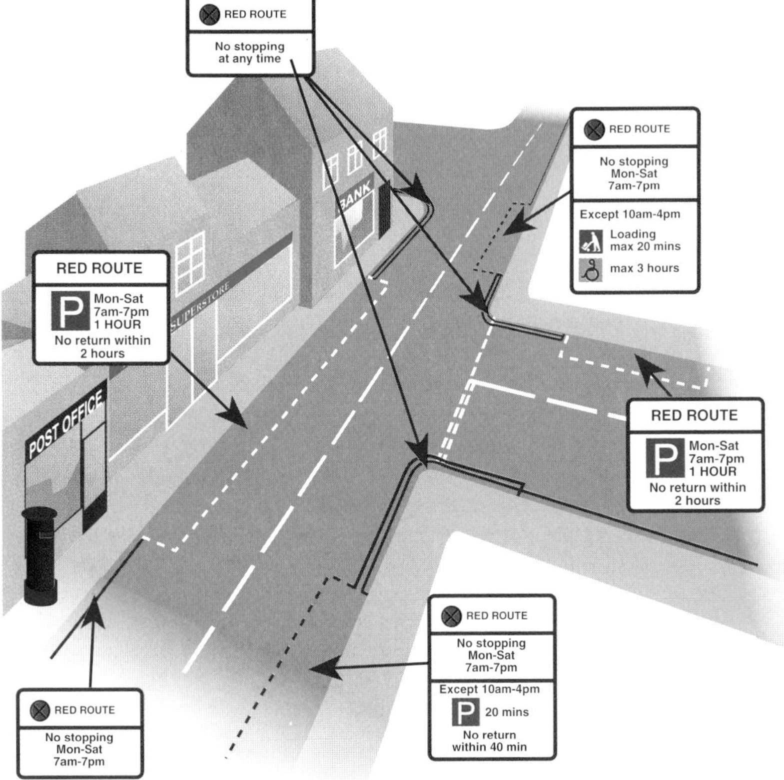

Red Route controls are enforced by Metropolitan Police traffic wardens. There's a fixed fine for illegal stopping on a Red Route, with no discounts for early payment.

The police or traffic wardens are able to provide limited dispensations for the rare occasions when it's necessary to load in a 'no stopping' zone. These will be available from the local police station.

There are five main types of Red Route controls.

**Double red lines** These ban all stopping 24 hours a day, seven days a week. You're not allowed to stop for

- Loading
- Dropping off passengers
- Visiting shops

'Loading' is defined as when a vehicle stops briefly to load or unload bulky or heavy goods. These goods must be heavy or bulky enough so that they can't be carried any distance and may involve more than one trip. If possible your vehicle should be parked legally and the goods carried to the premises. Picking up items that are able to be carried, like shopping, doesn't constitute loading.

**Single red lines** These ban all stopping during the daytime, such as 7 am to 7 pm Monday to Saturday. Outside these hours unrestricted stopping is allowed.

**Parking boxes** These allow vehicles free parking and can also be used for loading. Red boxes allow parking or loading outside rush hours such as between 10 am and 4 pm for either 20 minutes or an hour during the day. White boxes allow parking or loading at **any** time but the length of stay may be restricted to 20 minutes or an hour during the day. At other times, such as 7 pm to 7 am and on Sundays, unrestricted stopping is allowed in either type of parking box.

**Loading boxes** These mark the areas where only loading is allowed. Red boxes allow loading outside rush hours, such as between 10 am and 4 pm, for up to 20 minutes. White boxes allow loading at **any** time, but during the day the length of stay is restricted to a maximum of 20 minutes. At other times, such as between 7 pm and 7 am and on Sundays, unrestricted stopping is allowed in either type of loading box.

**Clearways** These are major roads where there's no need to stop. There will be no red lines but Red Route clearway signs will indicate that stopping isn't allowed at any time.

For more information on Red Routes contact the Traffic Director for London, College House, Great Peter Street, London SW1P 3LN.
Tel: 0171 222 4545.

## Bus lanes

Bus lanes are marked on busy roads to assist the flow of public transport. Use them sensibly and don't be tempted to speed just because the lane is clear ahead. You may be driving along the inside of stationary or slow-moving traffic where pedestrians could be tempted to cross the road. They may not be prepared for you moving faster along the bus lane.

Where the lane has been obstructed try not to get annoyed. It achieves nothing except to distract you from your driving.

Indicate in good time when you're ready to move out and wait patiently for an opportunity.

Be prepared for the end of the lane, where other traffic may be changing position.

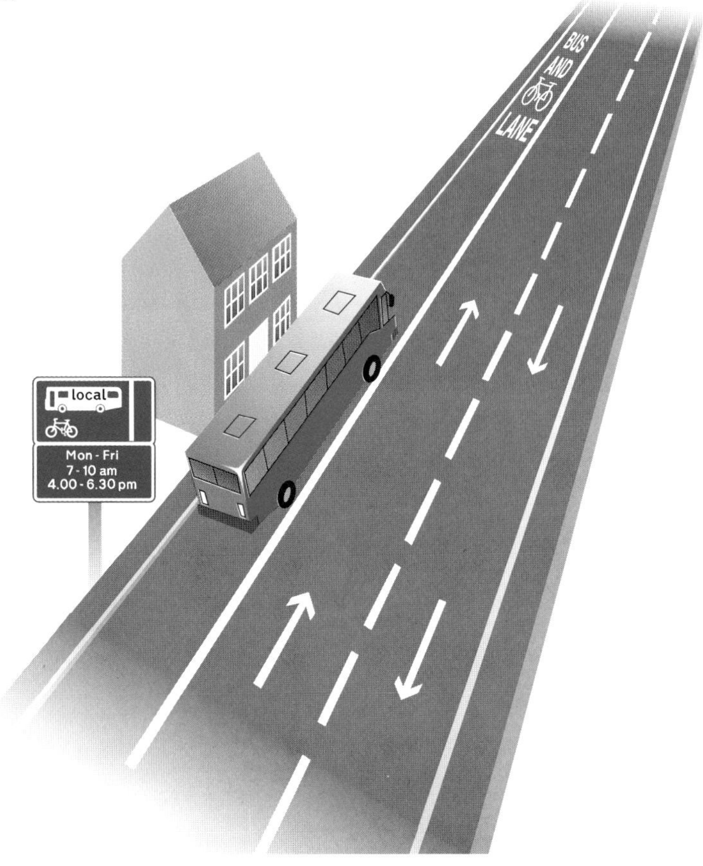

## Parking restrictions

Whenever you're driving, whether on stage carriage, on a private hire contract, on tour work, or whilst not in service, maintain your professionalism. Don't stop in places where

- Loading and unloading aren't allowed
- You'll cause an obstruction
- You'll inconvenience other road users

Similarly, don't park

- Where parking is prohibited
- Where there's a risk of theft or vandalism
- Less than 10 metres (33 feet) from any junction, wherever possible, unless there's an authorised parking space

## Route planning

Plan your route carefully. It's never advisable to take short cuts through residential or narrow streets to avoid traffic congestion: you may get stuck. In some towns weight, size and other vehicle restrictions prohibit you from leaving the main through routes and ring roads, except for access.

The Metropolitan Police operate an advisory service for coach operators. Their telephone number is at the back of this book.

## Your passengers

Various regulations cover how you should deal with passengers and their behaviour. Specific rules relate to

- The conduct of drivers, conductors, couriers and inspectors
- The number of passengers carried
- The carriage of schoolchildren
- The carriage and consumption of alcohol
- Smoking
- Passengers causing danger or offence by their behaviour or condition
- The carriage or use of dangerous, noxious or illegal substances by passengers

In addition to the legal obligations and restrictions, most operators require that specific rules must be followed. It's in your own interest to read and comply with them. You may risk dismissal if you don't.

## Health and Safety

A wide range of activities are covered by the Health and Safety regulations. These include

- Limits on the weight of objects that should be lifted manually (loading suitcases, etc.)
- Requirements for protective clothing when handling oils and other maintenance materials, and when disposing of waste (emptying toilet tanks, etc.)
- Safe operating procedures in the event of emergencies or breakdowns
- Safe working practices in garages, bus depots and bus stations

## Safe working practices

Every year someone in the bus and coach industry is killed or badly injured in an incident involving moving vehicles in confined spaces. When parking close to a wall or another vehicle make sure that

- You leave room for other vehicles
- You're not trapping or crushing anyone

Those vehicles fitted with air suspension may move a considerable amount when parked or when started, as air is exhausted or injected into the air bags. Parking one of these vehicles too close to a pillar, wall or another vehicle may cause damage or injury.

Vehicle maintenance and repair work isn't normally your responsibility. However, you should be able to recognise faults with your vehicle and fill in defect reports correctly. You may have to carry out minor emergency repairs on the road, when conditions dictate, but don't attempt anything beyond that. You shouldn't do any work on engines or any other vehicle components unless you're fully trained or supervised.

Be careful of the following hazards in workshops and garages

- Asbestos dust
- Paint spray
- Solvents
- Exhaust fumes
- Degreasing agents
- Inspection pits
- Moving/reversing vehicles
- Vehicle batteries
- Vehicle chair lifts or 'kneeling' mechanisms
- Bus washers

If you don't have to be in the workshop or garage, keep out.

The professional driving standards described in this book should also apply to drivers employed as 'shunters' or mechanics who drive buses and coaches as part of their job.

## Anti-theft measures

There are many anti-theft systems on the market, some which manufacturers are fitting as original equipment to vehicles.

This book isn't intended to provide a detailed description of the precautions that you can take to avoid having your vehicle stolen or broken into, except in general terms. To provide this information would only alert criminals to the ways in which they can be overcome.

Unless you're handing a vehicle over to another driver, or parking it on an operator's premises where it's safe to do so, don't

- Leave a vehicle unlocked or unattended
- Allow passengers to leave personal effects on board, except in locked luggage compartments
- Forget to set any fitted anti-theft devices

Remember, numerous incidents have occurred in the past when considerable damage was done after buses or coaches were driven away by unauthorised persons. Not only was there damage to an operator's vehicle, but also to those belonging to innocent parties.

The basic rules are simple

- Avoid carelessness
- Assess the risks of theft or damage
- Set all devices fitted

# PART THREE DRIVING SKILLS

This part looks at the professional driving skills you'll need to acquire to help you to deal with various road situations and weather conditions. It's concerned with the techniques you should use to look after yourself and your passengers.

## The topics covered

- Professional driving
- Driving at night
- Motorway driving
- All-weather driving
- Accidents and breakdowns

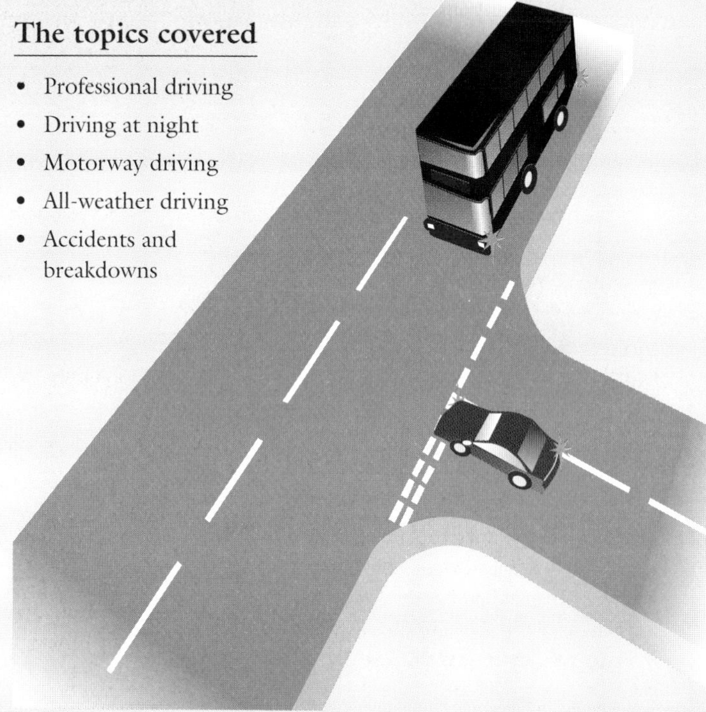

## Essential skills

Professional drivers adopt a positive approach to driving. This means

- Looking after yourself, your vehicle and your passengers
- Planning well ahead
- Practising good observation
- Keeping in control
- Anticipating events

Professional driving means making allowances. You must always consider the safety and comfort of passengers. Sometimes you'll have to allow for the ignorance of other road users. In most cases, they'll have very little idea of the problems a bus or coach driver faces when driving such a large vehicle.

### Control

It's essential that your vehicle is under control at all times. You must drive it skilfully and plan ahead, so that your bus is always travelling at the correct speed and ready for your next manoeuvre. You should never have to do anything at the last minute.

**If you get caught out, *you've* got it wrong.**

### Awareness

You need to develop your awareness, to know what's going on round you at all times. This can be achieved through

- Your memory of similar situations
- An understanding of what might happen
- The ability to plan ahead
- Anticipation – experience will soon tell you what other road users are probably going to do next
- Being in control. Plan your actions, don't be forced into situations by others

You must always drive

- Responsibly
- Carefully
- Considerately
- Courteously

Competition between different bus companies offers you a challenge. At all times, show that your standards are high and that you can drive a PCV with skill and safety.

## Anticipation

There aren't many excuses for being taken by surprise when you're driving. Almost every event is predictable.

You must consider and prepare for all possibilities in all situations, especially when you don't know what other road users intend to do. Remember, you won't be able to brake or swerve like lighter, smaller vehicles can.

Put yourself in other people's shoes. Make allowances for

- Children
- Cyclists
- Horse riders
- Elderly pedestrians
- Obviously less able drivers
- Learner drivers

Problems arise when you can't be sure of what vulnerable road users might do. Try to prepare yourself for all possibilities.

## Avoiding aggression

Your passengers trust you: their safety is in your hands once they board your bus. Don't betray that trust. When you're driving

- Accept that mistakes can be made
- Expect others to make mistakes
- Don't 'rise' to aggression

People who drive aggressively often see their driving as a competition. In every situation they feel the need to 'win'. It's preferable to let them go on their way. By doing so you'll have lost nothing. You're simply refusing to be involved in their bad driving behaviour – and their accident.

Your driving should always be a good example to others. By driving patiently and being prepared for the unexpected you'll avoid

- Giving offence to others
- Creating hostility
- Provoking others to drive dangerously

## Safe procedure

It may seem to other road users that coach drivers are 'racing' when one coach overtakes another. This is usually because of a coach's load or its speed limiter, and tends to be more obvious on hills.

Sometimes the bus being overtaken may be more powerful and the overtaking vehicle must drop back. If another coach has started to overtake you but appears to be unable to pass, be prepared to ease your own speed if you think that it would be safer for the other driver to move back to the left.

For this reason you must not drive in close convoy. If you're driving with other vehicles from the same company, don't drive nose-to-tail or look as though you're vying for position with each other along the road.

Competing with other drivers will eventually lead to you risking your own safety or that of your passengers and other road users.

## Effective observation

As a PCV driver, you'll often have a better view from your driving position than most other road users. However, because of your vehicle's size and design, it will have more blind spots than many smaller vehicles.

You must use the mirrors effectively and act upon what you see in them. Just looking isn't enough. You need to know what road users around you are doing, or might do next. Frequently check down the sides of your vehicle.

### Offside

- For overtaking traffic coming up behind, or already alongside
- Before signalling
- Before changing lanes, overtaking, moving or turning to the right

### Nearside

- For cyclists or motorcyclists 'filtering' up the nearside
- For traffic on your left when moving in two or more lanes
- To check when you've passed another road user, parked vehicle or pedestrians before moving back to the left
- To see where your wheels are in relation to the kerb or gutter
- Before changing lanes, after overtaking, before turning left or moving further to the left, leaving roundabouts

Constantly check offside, nearside, offside, and so on.

With a high seating position you must also be aware of pedestrians or cyclists. They may be out of sight below the windscreen line, directly in front of your vehicle. Check for them

- Before moving off
- At pedestrian crossings
- In slow-moving congested traffic
- When manoeuvring to park

### Blind spots

In addition, inside some coaches – particularly those with high side windows – it's difficult to see to either side. When you want to move off you should open the window and look down and round to the right to ensure that it's clear before you pull away.

Many modern vehicles are fitted with additional mirrors on the left-hand side, positioned so that the driver can observe the nearside front wheel in relation to the kerb. Use them whenever you're pulling in to park alongside the kerb, in addition to checking the vehicle's position when you have to move close to the left in normal driving.

Hitting the kerb or wandering onto a verge can seriously deflect the steering or damage the tyre, which could result in a blow-out later.

**Observation at junctions**

Despite your higher seating position there will still be some junctions where you can't see past parked vehicles or even road signs. If possible, try to look through the windows of other vehicles, or watch for other vehicles' reflections in shop windows, which can give you some valuable information.

If you still can't see any oncoming traffic you'll have to ease forward until you can see properly without emerging too far out into the path of approaching traffic. Remember, some road users are more difficult to see than others, particularly cyclists and motorcyclists.

- **L**ook
- **A**ssess
- **D**ecide before you
- **E**merge or enter, then
- **N**egotiate the junction

Avoid having to say, 'Sorry, but I didn't see you coming'.

**If you don't know, don't go.**

At junctions, check for everything that you would normally look for whenever you move off from a standstill position. For example, it can be difficult to predict what pedestrians might do at junctions. Sometimes they might run out into the road, or other times they might just step out without having seen you.

Never decide to go after just one quick glance. Take in the whole scene before you commit yourself to moving out.

- Think once
- Think twice
- Think bike

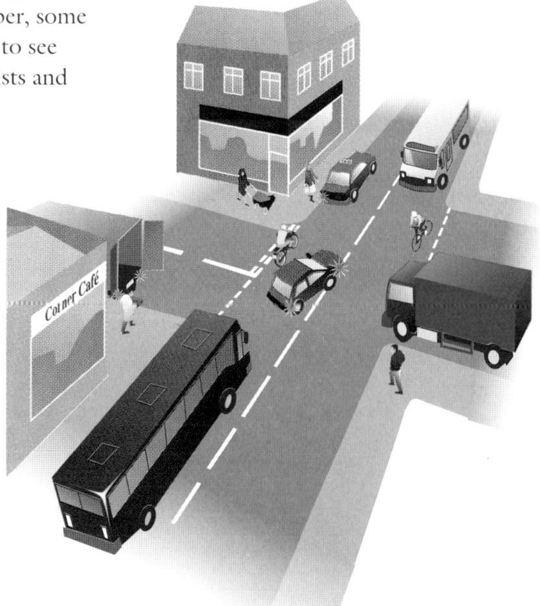

## Zones of vision

As a PCV licence-holder you must have better-than-average eyesight. To be a skilful driver you must watch the road ahead constantly, to see what's happening and to anticipate what might happen next.

You should already know what's behind and next to you. You also need to know what's happening at the edges of your vision and to note what's happening 'out of the corner of your eye'. You need to act on **all** your observations. Check for

- Vehicles about to come out of junctions
- Children running out
- Bikes and motorcycles
- Pedestrians stepping out

Look for clues. If you see a cyclist ahead glance round to the right they're probably going to try to turn right into the next road. Be ready for it. Similarly, watch the actions of pedestrians as they approach kerbs and cross the road. Elderly people sometimes become confused and change direction suddenly, or even turn back.

Keep a good look out for all horse riders. If the animal starts to behave nervously allow the rider time and space to control their mount. The noise of a bus's exhaust or brakes can disturb even a normally calm horse.

## Safe distances

Never drive at such a speed that you can't stop in the distance that you can see is clear ahead. You need to do this regardless of the weather, the road and whether you're carrying passengers or not. This is one rule of safe driving that must **never** be broken.

- Keep a safe separation distance between you and the vehicle in front
- In good weather conditions leave at least 1 metre (3 feet) per mph of your speed, or a two-second time gap
- On wet roads you'll need to leave at least a four-second time gap

### The 'two-second rule'

You can check the time gap easily. Watch the vehicle in front pass a stationary object such as a bridge, pole, sign, etc. and then say to yourself

**'Only a fool breaks the two-second rule.'**

You should have finished saying this by the time you reach the object. If you haven't, you're too close.

On some motorways this rule is drawn to drivers' attention by 'chevrons' painted on the road surface. The instruction 'Keep at least two chevrons from the vehicle ahead' also appears on a sign at these locations.

In busy, slow-moving traffic you may not need to leave as much space, but you must still leave enough distance in which to stop safely.

### Tailgating

If you find another vehicle driving too close behind you, gradually ease your speed to increase the gap between you and any vehicle ahead. You'll then be able to brake more gently and remove the likelihood of the close-following vehicle running into you from behind.

If another vehicle pulls into the safe separation gap you're leaving, ease off your speed to extend the gap again.

Never drive, at speed, within a few feet of the vehicle in front. It isn't only car drivers in motorway right-hand lanes who commit this offence. Lorry and bus drivers can sometimes be seen driving much too close behind another vehicle – often at normal motorway speeds. If anything unexpected happens, an accident could follow.

You must not rely on someone else to plan ahead for you. They may not possess the same skills as you. Always keep your distance.

## Being aware of others

Look well ahead for stop lights. On a road with the national speed limit in force or on the motorway, watch for hazard warning lights flashing. These show that traffic ahead is slowing down quickly.

When you plan well ahead less effort is needed to drive a bus. You should be able to keep your vehicle moving by anticipating traffic speeds. Your fuel economy should improve and this could help your company to stay competitive.

Before you change direction or speed you must decide how any change will affect other road users. It's important to know what's happening behind you as well as what's going on in front of you. Fast-moving cars or motorcycles can catch up with you surprisingly quickly.

Bus or coach drivers can't usually see much by looking round, which is why you must always be aware of vehicles just behind you and to either your left- or right-hand side as they come into your blind spot position.

A quick sideways glance is often helpful, especially

- Before changing lanes on a motorway or dual carriageway
- Where traffic joins from the right or the left
- Prior to merging from a motorway slip road

Don't take your attention off the road ahead for any longer than is absolutely necessary.

### Mirrors

You must use the mirrors well before you signal or make any manoeuvre, such as before

- Moving away
- Changing direction
- Turning left or right
- Overtaking
- Changing lanes
- Slowing or stopping
- Speeding up
- Opening any offside door

Mirrors must be

- Clean
- Properly adjusted
- Free from defects

Whenever you use the mirrors you must act sensibly on what you see. Take note of the traffic behind you and what it's doing.

**Looking isn't enough.**

## Traffic lights

At many busy road junctions the road is covered in skid marks. This shows that vehicles have come up to the junction too fast and have had to brake hard.

### Approaching traffic lights

**Lights on green** Ask yourself

- How long has green been showing?
- Can I stop safely at this speed if the lights change?
- If I do have to brake hard, will the traffic behind be able to stop safely?
- Are there any vehicles waiting to turn left or right?
- How will weather conditions affect my braking?

**Lights on red** You must, of course, stop at red traffic lights. However, you may be able to time your approach so that you keep your vehicle moving as they change. Timing your approach to avoid stopping and moving off again may make your driving easier and your passengers more comfortable.

**Lights not working** If you come up to traffic lights that aren't working, or there's a sign to show that they're out of order, treat the junction like an unmarked junction and drive with great care. Practise good, all-round observation and be prepared to stop if others assume priority.

**Lights 'stuck' on red** You shouldn't go through a red traffic light by law, unless a police officer tells you to do so. Occasionally, the signals may go out of phase and the red light shows for longer than it should. Remember, if you drive on and there's an accident, you'll have broken the law.

Never attempt to 'beat' any traffic lights. Don't

- Speed up to try to beat the signals. Remember what might happen to your passengers if you have to suddenly brake
- Leave it until the last moment to brake. Heavy braking may well end up in loss of control

A vehicle coming across your path may anticipate the lights changing and accelerate forward while the lights are still on red-and-amber. Don't take any risks.

## Giving signals

You should signal to

- Warn others about what you're going to do, especially if this involves a manoeuvre that isn't obvious to other road users
- Help other road users

Road users you need to consider include

- Drivers of oncoming vehicles
- Drivers of following vehicles
- Motorcyclists
- Cyclists
- Crossing supervisors
- Police directing traffic
- Pedestrians
- Horse riders

Give all signals clearly and in good time. Also, use only those signals that are shown in *The Highway Code*.

You should avoid giving any signals that could confuse, especially when you're going to pull up just past a road on the left. Another road user might misunderstand the meaning of the signal.

Avoid giving unauthorised signals, despite how widely you assume they're understood. This applies to headlight 'codes' and alternating indicator signals. Remember, any signal that doesn't appear in *The Highway Code* is unauthorised and could be misunderstood by another road user.

Avoid unnecessary signals. Always consider the effect your signal will have on all other road users.

### Using the horn

There are few instances when you'll need to use the horn. Using it doesn't

- Give you any 'right of way'
- Relieve you of the responsibility of driving safely

You should only sound the horn if you

- Think that another road user may not have seen you
- Need to warn other road users of your presence – at blind bends or a humpback bridge, for example

Don't use the horn

- To rebuke another road user
- Simply to attract attention (unless to avoid an accident)
- When stationary (unless a moving vehicle presents a danger)
- At night between 11.30 pm and 7 am in a built-up area, unless there's danger from a moving vehicle

Avoid any long blasts on the horn, which can alarm pedestrians. If they

## Problems encountered

You need extra skills to drive a bus, coach or minibus at night, especially over long distances. There are also additional responsibilities for the driver.

The problems related to driving at night are

- Poor visibility
- Less light (street lights or vehicle lights only)
- Dazzle from the headlights of oncoming vehicles
- Shadows created by patchy street lighting
- Poor lighting on other vehicles, pedal cycles, etc.
- Dangers created by getting tired

You must concentrate even harder than normal. The slightest distraction or break in your concentration can result in an accident. Fatal accidents have happened because the driver of a large vehicle either fell asleep briefly or didn't see an unlit broken-down truck or car until it was too late.

You need to plan long journeys at night, particularly on motorways where there's little to ease the boredom. You should also make sure that you get proper rest and refreshment stops.

Above all, you must drive at a speed that allows you to stop safely in the distance that you can see is clear ahead. In many cases, that's within the distance lit up by your headlights or by street lights.

## Tiredness

The smallest lapse of concentration at the wheel can result in loss of control. Many fatal accidents have been attributed to the driver becoming over-tired and falling asleep at the wheel. Remember

- Don't drive without proper rest periods
- Keep plenty of cool fresh air circulating through the driving area
- Don't allow the air around you to become too warm
- Avoid eating a heavy meal before or during a journey
- Pull up at the next safe convenient place if you feel your concentration slipping
- Listen to the radio or a tape if you can do so without disturbing your passengers. (Don't change tapes while driving, though.)
- Walk around in the fresh air before setting off again after a rest stop

## Night vision

Have your eyesight tested regularly and make sure that your night vision is up to the standard required. If in doubt, have it checked. Avoid

- Wearing tinted glasses
- Using windscreen or window tinting sprays

### Lighting-up time

Regardless of the official lighting-up times (when you must turn your lights on), you should be ready to switch on any lights that you may need. If the weather conditions are poor or it becomes overcast, don't be afraid to be the first driver to switch on. See and be seen.

### Unlit vehicles

Only vehicles under 1,525kg are allowed to park in 30 mph zones without lights at night time. Be on the alert when driving in built-up areas, especially when the street lighting is patchy.

Although builders' skips must be lit and show reflective plates to oncoming traffic, these items are often either forgotten or vandalised, so be on the lookout for skips.

## Adjusting to darkness

When you step out from a brightly lit area into darkness, such as when leaving a motorway service station, your eyes will take a short while to adjust to the dark conditions. Use this time to check and clean your lights, reflectors, lenses and mirrors.

## At dawn

Other drivers may have been driving through the night and may also be less alert. Leave your lights on until you're satisfied that other road users will see you.

Remember, it's harder to judge speed and distance correctly in the half-light at dusk and dawn. The colour of some vehicles makes them harder to see in half-light conditions. By switching your lights on you could avoid another road user stepping, riding or driving out into your path because they hadn't realised how close or how fast your vehicle was travelling.

**See and be seen.**

## Vehicle lighting

It's essential that all lights are clean and that the bulbs and light units work properly. As well as being able to see ahead properly, other road users must be able to recognise the size of your vehicle and which way it's going.

In general, white lights indicate that the vehicle is

- Moving towards you
- Stationary, facing you
- Reversing towards you (or is about to do so)

Red lights mean that the vehicle is

- Moving away from you
- Ahead of you and braking
- Stationary, facing away from you

Amber lights that aren't flashing mark the side of a vehicle.

### Auxiliary lighting

High-intensity rear fog lights and additional front fog lights must only be used when visibility is less than 100 metres (about 330 feet).

### Interior lights

You should also turn on the interior lights if it's gloomy during the day, as well as at night. It helps passengers to move about the bus more easily and safely.

Coaches may have special lighting for night use. Never leave the interior of your coach in darkness when you have passengers aboard.

Interior lights have another role in road safety. Newer buses have marker lights along the side to ensure that they're visible as they emerge from junctions, etc. Remember, a well-lit bus interior is even easier to see.

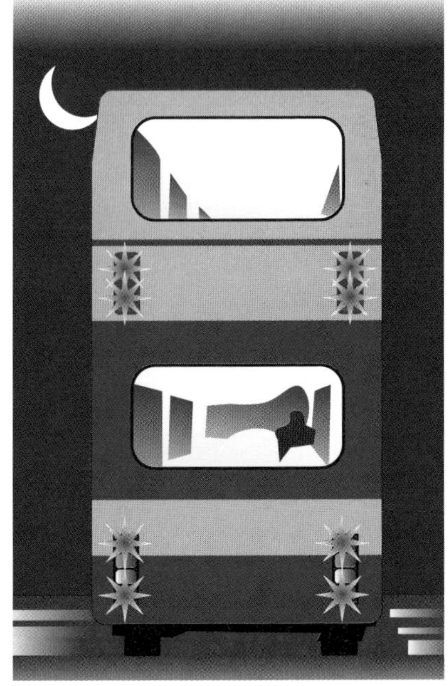

### Parked vehicles

All buses, coaches and most minibuses – depending on their weight – must have lights on when parked on the road at night.

Even though a lay-by is generally very close to the carriageway you must still have your lights on. Unless your vehicle is parked 'off street', such as in a coach park, by law it must be clearly lit.

You must park on the left-hand side of the road unless you're on a one-way street and it's safe to park on the right-hand side of the road.

## Driving in built-up areas

Always use dipped headlights in built-up areas at night. It helps others to see you and also aids your visibility if the street lighting changes or isn't working properly.

Watch out for

- Pedestrians in dark clothing
- Joggers
- Cyclists (often without lights)

Take extra care when approaching pedestrian crossings. Drive at such a speed that you can stop safely if necessary.

Make sure that you still obey the speed limits even if the roads appear to be empty.

### Maintenance work

Remember that essential maintenance work is often carried out at night time. Street cleansing in the larger cities often takes place at night, so be on the lookout for slow-moving vehicles.

Be on the alert for diversion signs, obstructions, coned-off sections of road, etc., which may be difficult to see at night.

## Driving in rural areas

If there's no oncoming traffic you should use full beam headlights to see as far ahead as possible. Dip your lights as soon as you see the lights of traffic coming towards you. This will avoid dazzling the oncoming driver or rider.

If there's no footpath, watch out for pedestrians on the nearside. *The Highway Code* advises pedestrians to walk facing oncoming traffic in these situations.

Be prepared for temporary traffic lights on rural roads.

## Fog at night

If fog is forecast at night **don't drive**. You'll be a serious hazard to other traffic if the fog becomes so thick that you're unable to go any further safely. Because of the difficulties of getting a bus or coach off the road in thick fog it's better not to start out in the first place.

If you start your journey when there's fog about and you're delayed, you'll be committing an offence if you drive for more than your permitted hours. After all, the delay was foreseeable.

Seriously reduced visibility has, unfortunately, resulted in a number of major incidents involving multi-vehicle pile-ups. If conditions become severe enough scheduled journeys may have to be cancelled. There's ample justification for putting caution before inconvenience.

## Overtaking at night

Because PCVs can take some considerable time to overtake other vehicles, you must only attempt to overtake when you can see well ahead that it's safe to do so.

This means that, unless you're driving on a dual carriageway or motorway you'll have few opportunities to overtake. Unless there's street lighting, you might not be able to see properly if there are bends, junctions, hills, etc., which may prevent you from seeing an oncoming vehicle.

If you do decide to overtake make sure that you can do so without 'cutting in' on the vehicle you're overtaking, or causing oncoming vehicles to brake or swerve. Also, never come up close behind another vehicle before you attempt to overtake it.

When overtaking, switch to main beam headlights when you're alongside to improve your vision ahead, provided this won't dazzle approaching traffic (on a dual carriageway, for instance).

### Using the correct beam

Don't drive so close to the vehicle in front that your lights dazzle the other driver. Make sure that you use the dipped beam when following another vehicle.

If another vehicle overtakes you, dip your headlights as soon as the vehicle starts to pass you. Your headlight beam should fall short of the vehicle in front.

## Breakdowns

If your vehicle breaks down try to stop as far to the left as possible. If you can, get off the main carriageway without causing danger or inconvenience to other road users, especially pedestrians.

Move your passengers as far forward in the vehicle as you can. This should help to limit injuries if another vehicle runs into the back of yours.

Place a warning cone, pyramid or reflective triangle at least 50 metres (165 feet) behind the vehicle on normal roads or 150 metres (492 feet) on motorways. It's essential to warn other traffic of the obstruction caused by your vehicle if an electrical problem has stopped the rear lights and hazard warning flashers from working.

Some foreign-built buses and coaches have outside fuse and relay boxes on the right-hand side of the vehicle. Don't attempt to work on the right-hand side of the vehicle unless protected by a recovery vehicle with flashing amber beacons. Even then, take great care on roads carrying fast-moving traffic. Many accidents happen at breakdowns. Protect yourself, your passengers and your vehicle.

### Assessing the dangers

If your vehicle is creating an obstruction or is a potential danger to other road users tell the police as soon as possible. This is particularly important if your vehicle is carrying passengers, especially schoolchildren. Their safety must come first.

If you think that there's a serious risk of collision, escort your passengers off the bus. Ensure that they wait somewhere well away from the traffic. Explain carefully what you're doing and ask people to go for help if necessary.

Make sure that you

- Know where all your passengers are
- Know what they're doing
- Keep them informed

Don't leave them, unless absolutely necessary.

**Don't ignore danger signals** If you suspect that there's something wrong with your vehicle don't be tempted to carry on driving. You could end up causing traffic jams if your bus eventually breaks down in an awkward place.

A minor problem could turn out to have major effects. For example, a broken injector pipe dripping fuel onto a hot exhaust manifold may only seem to be a slight engine hesitation to the driver. However, this problem has been known to cause fires in which the vehicle was completely destroyed.

### Recovery agencies

If you're driving long distances on overnight services you must know what to do if you break down and require

- A replacement vehicle for your passengers
- The attendance of a breakdown vehicle and/or recovery

If you're an operator, even if you have only one vehicle, you must be prepared for anything that might happen. Under no circumstances must passengers be left stranded.

Vehicles that break down on the motorway must be removed promptly for safety reasons.

## Basic preparation

Accident records show that, statistically, motorways are the safest roads in the UK. However, motorway accidents often involve several fast-moving vehicles and consequently result in more serious injuries and damage than accidents on other roads.

Because of the high numbers of large vehicles using motorways many of these accidents involve lorries and, occasionally, coaches and minibuses. But if everyone who used the motorway drove to the same high standard as PCV drivers, it's arguable that many of these incidents could be avoided.

There's often little room for error when driving at speed on a motorway. The generally higher speeds and the volume of traffic mean that conditions can change much more quickly on motorways than on other roads. Because of this you need to be

- Totally alert
- Physically fit
- Concentrating fully
- Assessing well ahead

If you aren't, you may fail to react quickly enough to any sudden change in traffic conditions.

### Fitness

Don't drive if you're

- Tired
- Feeling ill
- Taking medicines that could affect your driving
- Unable to concentrate for any reason

Any of these factors could affect your reactions, especially in an emergency.

### Rest periods

You must take the compulsory rest periods in your driving schedule. On long journeys, try to plan them to coincide with a stop at a motorway service area. This is especially important at night, when a long journey can make you more tired than usual.

If you eat a large meal immediately before driving, the combined effects of a warm coach, the constant drone of the engine and long boring stretches of road, especially at night, can soon cause the onset of drowsiness. Falling asleep at the wheel can happen as easily as that. Don't let it happen to you.

It's against the law to stop anywhere on the motorway or on its hard shoulder or slip roads for a rest. A driver's tiredness is foreseeable and isn't considered to be an emergency.

If you start to feel even slightly tired, open the windows, turn the heating down and get off the motorway at the next junction. Even if you aren't scheduled to stop, it's preferable to falling asleep at the wheel.

When you reach a service area have a hot drink, wash your face (to refresh yourself) and walk round in the fresh air before driving on.

### Regulations

You must follow the special motorway rules and regulations. Study the sections in *The Highway Code* that relate to motorways. Know, understand and obey any warning signs and signals.

## Vehicle checks

Motorway driving usually involves driving long distances at sustained high speeds. Before you drive on the motorway you must make your usual checks, but the following merit particular attention.

### Tyres

All the tyres must be in good condition and be properly inflated. Some motorways are littered with the remains of tyres that disintegrated during long high-speed running.

Surveys have shown that the tyres that are most likely to fail are those which are over-inflated. Make sure that the pressures are checked regularly, as you can't tell simply by looking at the tyre. Inspect both the inside and outside walls and the treads for signs of wear, damage, bulges, separation, exposed cords, etc.

Make sure that your vehicle has the specified sized wheels and tyres fitted. Smaller wheels will rotate faster and may overheat on longer journeys. Some PCVs are designed to have different sized wheels on the front and the rear, but sizes should never be mixed on the same axle.

Ensure that all tyres are suitable for the loads being carried and the speeds driven. Commercial lorry tyres aren't always suitable for PCVs. You should always consult tyre specialists who will explain the ratings marked on each tyre.

Check for excessive heat when you stop for a break. It's surprising how many large vehicles can be seen travelling fast with the driver apparently oblivious to a tyre shredding itself in a cloud of smoke. Use the mirrors to check your tyres while you drive.

### Mirrors

Ensure that all mirrors are properly adjusted to give the best possible view to the rear. Also, make sure that they're clean. The simple device of tying a piece of cloth to the mirror bracket causes the air flow to 'wipe' the mirror and effectively clean it. Purpose-made devices are available, which do the same job but look more acceptable.

In winter, make full use of any demisting heating elements fitted to your mirrors.

Keep the lenses and screens of any rear-view video equipment clean and clear.

### Windscreen

All glass must be

- Clean
- Clear
- Free from defects

Keep all windscreen washer reservoirs topped up and the jets clear. Make sure that all wiper blades are in good condition.

Don't hang mascots or put stickers where they could restrict your view. They'll distract you at first, but when you get used to them they could cause something unusual outside the coach to go unnoticed.

Certain specified minor defects in a windscreen are accepted for vehicle tests, but the only really safe option is to have the windscreen repaired by an approved specialist or to have a replacement fitted as soon as possible. The effects of a coach windscreen breaking inwards at speed are devastating, so don't risk it.

### Spray-suppression equipment

It's essential that you check all spray-suppression equipment fitted to the vehicle before setting out, especially if bad weather is expected. If wheel arches have sections of anti-spray fitments missing report it as a defect.

### Instruments

Check all gauges, especially any warning lights – air, oil pressure, coolant, etc.

### Lights and indicators

By law, all lights must be in working order even in daylight. Make sure that all bulbs, headlight units, lenses and reflectors are fitted, clean and working properly.

High-intensity rear fog lights and marker lights (if fitted) must also work correctly. Indicator lights must flash between 60 and 120 times per minute. Reversing lights must either work automatically when reverse gear is chosen or be switched on from the cab, with a warning light to show when they're on.

### Fuel

Make sure that you either have enough fuel on board to complete the journey or have the facility (cash, agency card, etc.) to refuel at a service area.

### Oil and coolant

The engine operates at sustained high speeds on a motorway so it's vital to check all oil levels before setting out. Running low can result in costly damage to the engine and could cause a breakdown at a dangerous location. Similarly, it's essential to check the levels of coolant in the system.

### Audio and video equipment

Don't allow the use of equipment to distract you from driving carefully and safely. You shouldn't use microphones or change radio stations or tapes whilst driving. If your bus is fitted with a communications radio or telephone you should only use it whilst driving if it's fitted with a 'hands off' microphone. Otherwise find a safe place to stop before using a hand-held one.

Any video or television screen fitted to your coach and used whilst driving shouldn't be

- Visible to you whilst you're driving
- Seen from outside the vehicle

To prevent other road users from seeing the screens you must ensure that curtains are pulled across the windows when televisions are being used.

## Joining a motorway

There are three ways in which traffic can join a motorway. All these entrances will be clearly signed.

### At a roundabout

The motorway exit from a roundabout will be signposted to prevent traffic that doesn't want to use the motorway from driving onto it unintentionally.

### Main trunk road becoming a motorway

There will be obvious advance warning signs so that prohibited traffic can leave the road before the motorway regulations come into force.

### Via a slip road

Slip roads leading directly onto the motorway will be clearly signed. Traffic that doesn't want or isn't permitted to use the motorway must act on these signs to avoid entering by mistake. In many cases the slip road begins as an exit from a roundabout.

**Effective observation** Before joining the motorway from a slip road try to assess the traffic conditions on the motorway itself. You may be able to do this as you approach from a distance or if, before joining it, you have to cross the motorway by means of an over-bridge.

Get as much advance information as you can to help you to plan your speed on the slip road before reaching the acceleration lane. You must give way to traffic already on the main carriageway. Plan your approach so that you don't have to stop at the end of the acceleration lane. Never use the size or speed of your vehicle to force your way onto the motorway.

Use the MSM/PSL routine. A quick sideways glance may be necessary to ensure that you correctly assess the speed of any traffic approaching in the nearside lane. Remember

- **L**ook for approaching traffic
- **A**ssess the speed of approaching vehicles
- **D**ecide when you can build up speed
- **E**merge safely onto the main carriageway
- **N**egotiate the hazard – adjust to the speed of traffic already on the motorway

Don't

- Pull out into the path of traffic in the nearside lane if this would cause it to slow down or swerve
- Drive along the hard shoulder to 'filter' in to the left-hand lane

At a small number of locations traffic merges onto the motorway from the right. Take extra care in these situations.

## Making progress

### Approaching access points

After passing a motorway exit there will usually be an entrance onto the motorway. Look well ahead and, if there are several vehicles joining the motorway

- Don't try to race them while they're in the acceleration lane
- Be prepared to adjust your speed
- Move to the next lane, if it's safe to do so, to allow joining traffic to merge

### Lane discipline

Keep to the left-hand lane unless you're overtaking slower vehicles. Buses and coaches that are fitted with speed limiters set to a maximum speed of 100 kph (62 mph) may not use the right-hand lane(s) on motorways with more than two lanes (for an initial trial period of two years from 1 January 1996), unless there are roadworks and signs direct otherwise. You must make sure that you know about any changes that may be introduced.

On two-lane motorways, all vehicles may use the right-hand lane for overtaking.

On a three- or four-lane motorway, make sure that you check for any vehicle in the right-hand lane(s) that might be about to move back to the left. Because you're driving a large vehicle some of the traffic coming up behind may be travelling at a much higher speed.

Look well ahead to plan any overtaking manoeuvre, especially given the effect a speed limiter will have on the power available to you. Watch out for signs showing a crawler lane for LGVs. This will suggest a long, gradual gradient ahead.

Use the MSM/PSL routine well before you signal to move out. Don't start to pull out and then signal, or signal at the same time as you begin the manoeuvre. Other drivers need time to react.

Don't allow your vehicle to 'wander', however slightly, before changing lanes. A PCV takes up most of the room available in a lane. You may cause an overtaking driver or rider to think that you're starting to pull out into their path if you move away from the middle of a lane.

Take special care if you're moving into the centre lane. You must be sure that another vehicle isn't planning to use the same road space.

If a very large slow-moving vehicle is being escorted watch for any signal by the police officers in the escort vehicle at the rear. You might need to move into the right-hand lane to pass it.

If a motorway lane merges from the right (this only happens in a few places) you should move over to the left as soon as it's safe to do so. The MSM/PSL routine must be used, with careful checks in the left-hand mirror and constant awareness of vehicles in the blind spots.

## Separation distance

When driving at motorway speeds you must allow more time for everything that you do. Allow

- Greater safety margins than on normal roads
- A safe separation distance

In good conditions that means you'll need at least

- 1 metre (about 3 feet) for every mph
- A two-second time gap

In poor conditions you'll need at least

- Double the distance
- A four-second time gap

In snow or icy conditions the stopping distances can be up to **ten** times those needed in normal dry conditions.

## Seeing and being seen

Make sure that you start out with a clean windscreen, mirrors and windows. Use the washers, wipers and demisters to keep the screen clear. In poor conditions use dipped headlights.

Keep reassessing traffic conditions around you. Watch out for brake lights or hazard flashers that show the traffic ahead is either stationary or slowing down. (Hazard flashers may be used on moving vehicles to alert traffic to danger ahead.)

High-intensity rear fog lights must only be used when visibility falls below less than 100 metres (about 330 feet). They should be switched off when visibility improves, unless fog is patchy and danger still exists.

## Motorway signs and signals

Motorway signs are larger than most normal road signs. They can be read from further away and can help you to plan ahead.

Make sure that you know where you're going and how you're going to get there. You must be ready in good time, well before reaching the exit that you need to use.

Where there are major roadworks there may be diversions for large vehicles. Look for the yellow

- Square
- Diamond
- Circle
- Triangle

symbols and follow the symbol on the route signs.

### Signals

Warning lights show when there are dangers ahead such as

- Accidents
- Fog
- Icy roads

Look out for variable message warning signs, which will warn you about

- Lane closures
- Speed limits
- Hazards
- Traffic stopped ahead

### Red light signals

If the red X signals show on the gantries above your lane don't go any further in that lane.

- Be ready to change lanes
- Be ready to leave the motorway
- Watch out for brake lights and hazard warning lights showing that traffic has stopped or is moving very slowly ahead

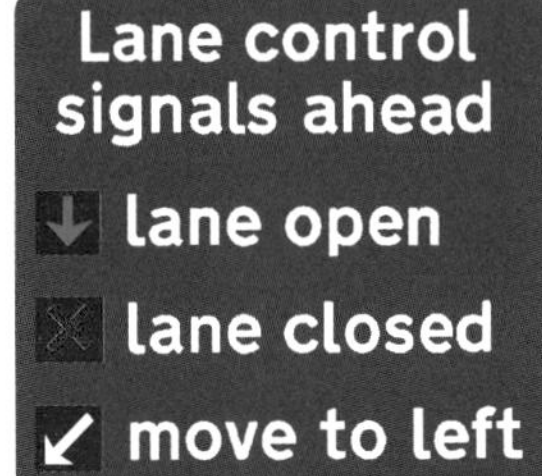


If the matrix sign indicating 'Stop, all lanes ahead closed' shows over every lane, stop and wait. You may not be able to see the reason for the signals and other drivers may be ignoring them. Remember, you're a professional driver who should know what the signals mean and can demonstrate to other drivers what they should do.

**React in good time.**

## Weather conditions

Because of the higher speeds on motorways, it's important to remember the effects that the weather can have on driving conditions.

### Crosswinds

Be aware of the effects of strong crosswinds on other road users. In particular, watch out for these effects

- After passing motorway bridges
- On high, exposed sections of road
- When passing vehicles towing caravans, horse boxes, etc.

If you're driving a high-sided vehicle, such as a double-decker or a high-floor coach, take notice of the warnings for drivers of such vehicles. Avoid known problem areas such as viaducts and high suspension bridges, if possible.

Motorcyclists are especially vulnerable to severe crosswinds on motorways. Watch out for them. Allow plenty of room when overtaking and check the left-hand mirror after you've overtaken them.

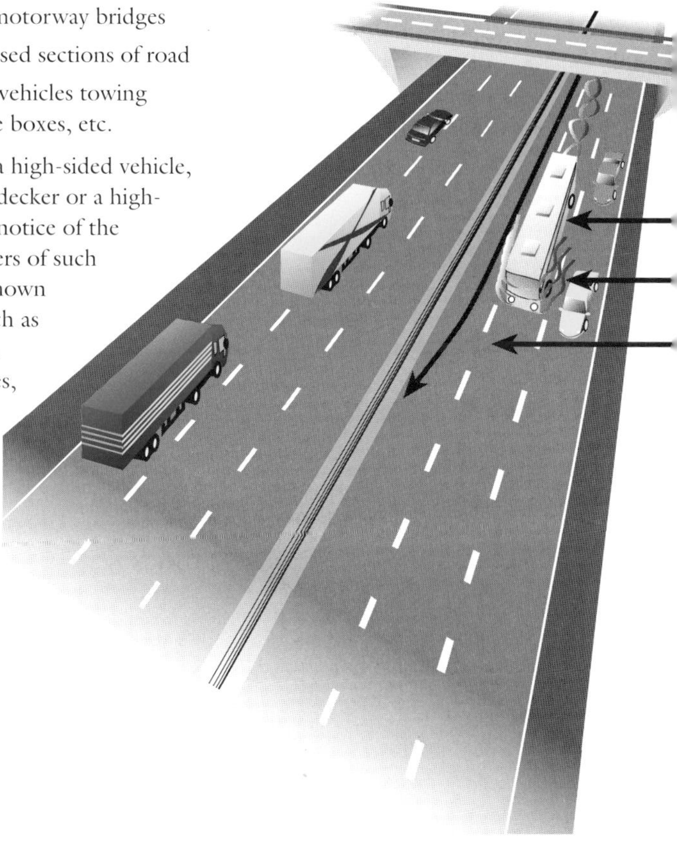

## Rain

The spray thrown up by large, fast-moving vehicles can make it very difficult to see ahead.

- Use headlights so that other drivers can see you
- Reduce speed when the road surface is wet. You need to be able to stop in the distance that you can see is clear
- Leave a greater separation gap. Remember the four-second rule as a minimum
- Make sure that all spray-suppression equipment fitted to your vehicle is working

Take extra care when the surface is still wet after rain. Roads can still be slippery even if the sun's out.

## Ice or frost

In cold weather, especially at night when temperatures can drop suddenly, watch out for any feeling of 'lightness' in the steering (not always obvious with power steering). This may suggest frost or ice on the road. Watch for signs of frost along the hard shoulder. Remember, a warm coach interior can isolate you from the real conditions outside.

Motorways that appear wet may in fact be frozen. There are devices that fix onto an outside mirror to show when the temperature drops below freezing point. Also, some manufacturers fit ice-alert warning lights on the instrument panel.

Allow up to **ten** times the normal distance for braking in these conditions. And remember, all braking must be gentle.

## Fog

Even if the motorway matrix signal doesn't show the word 'Fog', use your own eyes. If there's fog on the motorway you must slow down so that you can stop in the distance that you can see is clear. You should

- Use dipped headlights
- Use the rear high-intensity fog lights if visibility is less than 100 metres (about 330 feet)
- Stay back
- Check your speedometer

Don't

- Speed up again if the fog is patchy. You could quickly run into dense fog again
- Hang onto the rear lights of the vehicle in front

Fog affects your judgement of speed and distance. You may be travelling faster than you think.

**Slow down.**

Multiple pile-ups on motorways don't just happen – they're caused by drivers who

- Travel too fast
- Drive too close
- Assume nothing has stopped ahead
- Ignore signals, or the obvious

**You can't know what's happening ahead if you can't see.**

Watch out for any signals that tell you to leave the motorway. Also, look for accidents ahead and for emergency vehicles coming up behind (possibly on the hard shoulder). Police cars may be parked on the hard shoulder with their lights flashing. This might mean that traffic has stopped on the carriageway ahead.

'Motorway Madness' is the term used to describe the behaviour of those reckless drivers who drive too fast for the conditions. After an accident it's too late to say, 'I just couldn't pull up in time to avoid hitting them!' The police prosecute drivers after serious multiple accidents. This is to get the message across to all drivers that they must

**Slow down in fog.**

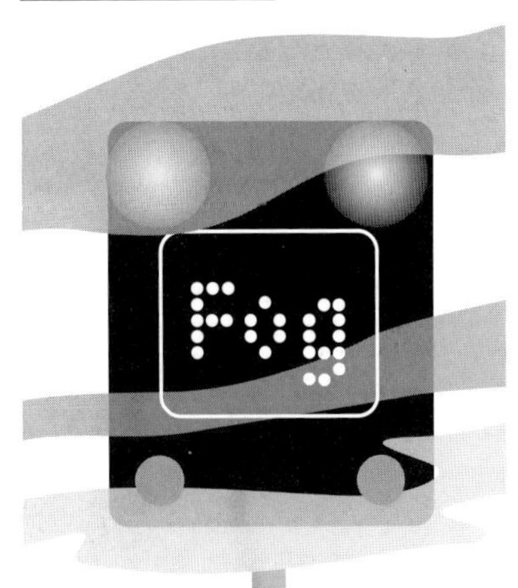

## Contraflows and roadworks

Essential roadworks involving two-way traffic on one carriageway of the motorway are called contraflow systems. The object is to let traffic carry on moving while repairs or resurfacing take place on the other carriageway or lanes.

Red and white marker posts are used to separate opposite streams of traffic. The normal white lane-marking reflective studs are replaced by temporary yellow/green fluorescent studs.

A 50 mph compulsory speed limit is usually in force in contraflow systems. Thus, in the event of a head-on collision the closing speed will be about 100 mph.

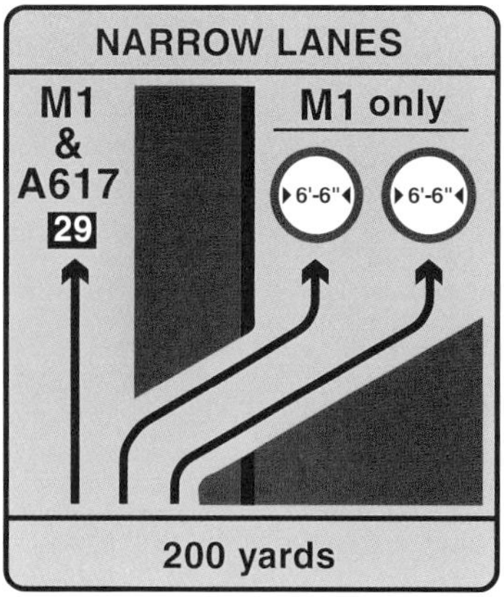

NARROW LANES
M1 & A617 29
M1 only
6'-6"
6'-6"
200 yards

- Concentrate on what's happening ahead
- Don't let the activity on the closed section distract you
- Don't break the speed limit
- Keep a safe separation distance from the vehicle in front
- Look well ahead to avoid having to brake hard
- Obey advance warning signs that tell you which lanes must not be used by large vehicles
- Avoid sudden steering movements or any need to brake sharply
- Don't change lanes if signs tell you to stay in your lane
- Don't speed up until the end of the roadworks and normal motorway speed limits apply again

### Signs

Take notice of advance warning signs (often starting five miles before the roadworks). Get into the correct lane in good time and don't force your way in at the last moment.

### Breakdowns

If your vehicle breaks down in the roadworks section stay with it. These sections of motorway are usually under TV monitoring, so a recovery vehicle (free within the roadworks section) will be with you as soon as possible.

Watch out for broken-down vehicles blocking the road ahead.

## Breakdowns on the motorway

- Try to get the vehicle as far to the left as possible
- Don't try to carry out minor repairs on the motorway
- Place a warning triangle or cone on the hard shoulder about 150 metres (492 feet) behind the vehicle
- Switch on the hazard warning lights
- Make sure that the vehicle lights are on at night, unless there's an electrical problem. If that's the case, ensure that your vehicle is visible in some other way (e.g., ask another motorist to park behind you)

### Emergency telephones

Motorway emergency telephones are free to use. You'll be connected directly to the motorway police control centre, who will then get in touch with a recovery company for you.

In most cases the emergency telephones are 1.6 km (about 1 mile) apart. The direction of the nearest phone will be shown by the arrow on the marker posts along the edge of the hard shoulder. Don't cross the carriageway or any slip road to get to a telephone. Face the oncoming traffic while using the telephone.

If your vehicle has its own telephone make sure that whoever you contact also informs the motorway police, or telephone them yourself.

If anything falls from either your vehicle or another vehicle

- Use the MSM routine and pull up safely on the hard shoulder at the next emergency telephone
- Use the emergency telephone to report it to the police
- Await the arrival of a police patrol

Don't

- Reverse
- Stop on the carriageway
- Attempt to recover the object yourself
- 'Wave' traffic down

## Leaving the motorway

Progressive signs will show upcoming exits. At one mile you'll see the

- Junction number
- Road number
- One-mile indicator

Half a mile from the exit you'll see signs for the

- Main town or city served by the exit
- Junction number
- Road number
- Half-mile exit

Finally, 300 yards (270 metres) before the exit there will be three countdown markers every 100 yards.

Remember, the driver of a vehicle travelling at 60 mph has 60 seconds from the one-mile sign to the exit. Even at a speed of 50 mph there's still only 80 seconds from the one-mile sign to the exit.

Plan well ahead in order to be in the left-hand lane in good time. Large vehicles in the left-hand lane may prevent a driver in the second lane from seeing the one-mile sign, leaving very little time to move to the left safely.

You must use the MSM/PSL routine in good time before changing lanes or signalling. Assess the speed of traffic well ahead. Avoid the situation where you try to overtake but then have to pull back in quickly in order to slow down to leave the motorway at the next exit. Don't

- Pull across the carriageway at the last moment
- Drive over the white chevrons that divide the slip road from the main carriageway

If you miss the exit that you wanted to take, drive on to the next one.

Occasionally there are several exits close together or a service area close to an exit. Look well ahead and plan your exit in good time. Watch out for other drivers' mistakes, especially those who leave it too late to exit from the motorway safely.

### Traffic queuing

In some places traffic can be held up on the slip road. Look well ahead and be prepared for this. Don't queue on the hard shoulder.

Illuminated signs have been introduced at a number of these sites to give advance warning of traffic queuing on the slip road or in the first lane. Watch out for indicators and hazard warning lights when traffic is held up ahead. Use the MSM/PSL routine in good time and move to the second lane if you aren't leaving at such an exit.

## End of the motorway

There are 'End of motorway' regulations signs

- At the end of slip roads
- Where the road becomes a normal main road

End
of motorway
regulations

These remind you that different rules apply to the road that you're joining. Watch out for signs advising you of

- Speed limits
- Dual carriageways
- Two-way traffic
- Clearways
- Motorway link roads
- Part-time traffic signals

### Reduce speed

After driving on the motorway for some time it's easy to become accustomed to the speed. When you first leave the motorway, 40 or 45 mph seems more like 20 mph. You should

- Adjust your driving to the new conditions as soon as possible
- Check the speedometer to see your actual speed

Start reducing speed when you're clear of the main carriageway. Remember, motorway slip or link roads often have sharp curves that need to be taken at lower speeds.

Look well ahead for traffic queuing at a roundabout or traffic signals. Be prepared for the change in traffic at the end of the motorway. Watch out for pedestrians, cyclists, etc.

Passengers want to travel 24 hours a day, 365 days a year. Whatever the weather, you'll need to drive safely so that you, your passengers and your vehicle arrive safely at your destination, with as few hold-ups as possible.

You must take notice of weather forecasts when warnings of severe weather, especially high winds, floods, fog and, above all, snow or blizzard conditions, are given. If a bus or coach gets stuck the road may well be blocked for essential rescue and medical services, putting large numbers of people at risk. In fog other vehicles could run into your vehicle if you stop or have left it unlit.

To drive in bad weather, training and preparation are vital. Only foolish drivers go out in poor conditions without being properly prepared. If the weather is really bad cancel or postpone your journey.

## Your vehicle

Your vehicle must be in good condition at all times. This means regular safety checks and strict observance of maintenance schedules. Far too many cases brought before a Licensing Authority result from incidents caused by a vehicle that wasn't looked after properly. Make sure that the vehicle you drive is fully roadworthy.

### Tyres

Check the tread depth and pattern. Examine tyres for cuts, damage or signs of cord visible at the side walls.

### Brakes

It's essential that the brakes are operating correctly. This is especially important on wet, icy or snow-covered roads. Any imbalance could cause a skid if the brakes are applied on a slippery surface. If your vehicle has an ABS make sure that you understand its use on slippery surfaces.

### Oil and fuel

Use the correct grades of fuel and oil in very hot or very cold weather.

Long periods of hot weather will make the oil in engines and turbochargers work harder. You should always allow engines with turbos fitted to idle for about a minute before increasing engine revs above tick-over speed (when starting) or before stopping the engine. This prevents the bearings from being starved of oil.

In extremes of cold you'll have to use either diesel fuel 'anti-waxing' additives or a suitable grade of diesel fuel with these properties to stop fuel lines freezing up.

Use of the correct coolant when topping up prevents dilution of the rust inhibitors and antifreeze components of the liquid. Also, remember that allowing a cooling system to freeze will wreck components and possibly crack the engine block or cylinder heads.

## Icy weather

Ensure that the whole of the windscreen is clear before you drive away in frosty conditions. Make full use of all heaters and demisters fitted.

If you're driving at night, remember that falling temperatures may lead to the formation of ice. This will cause ungritted roads to become very slippery. If the steering feels light you're probably driving on ice. Ease your speed as soon as you can. All braking must be gentle and over much longer distances.

Leave more time for the journey because you'll need to drive more slowly than usual. On slippery surfaces, keep a safe separation distance from any vehicle in front. Allow **ten** times the normal stopping distance.

Drive sensibly and be careful of other road users getting into difficulties. Don't accelerate, brake or steer suddenly. No risks are ever justified.

**If conditions are really bad, don't drive.**

## Heavy rain

You must make sure that you can see clearly ahead at all times. Don't drive if a windscreen wiper is faulty, even though many PCVs have more than one pair of wipers. In addition, the windscreen must be demisted fully and the windscreen washer bottle(s) topped up with the correct washing fluid. This is particularly important in winter. It's against the law to drive with frozen or ineffective windscreen washers.

Allow more space for braking – at least twice as much as in dry conditions. If possible, brake only when the vehicle's stable (and preferably when travelling in a straight line). Also, avoid sudden or hard braking.

Obey advisory speed limit signs on motorways.

Other road users will have more difficulty seeing when there's heavy rain and spray so make sure that all spray-suppression equipment on your vehicle is secure and working correctly.

Don't use rear fog lights unless visibility is less than 100 metres (330 feet). Fog lights reflect and dazzle following drivers.

### Mud

Take care when driving on off-road sites, such as at rallies, showgrounds, festivals, etc. If you get stuck there's very limited scope to 'rock' your PCV out of ruts (as you might with a car). Clearance underneath is often so limited that the exhaust could be ripped off, even if the vehicle has sunk as little as four or five inches. Seek assistance before this happens.

A bar from another vehicle on hard standing or the use of a winch may recover the situation without damage. Once the vehicle has sunk in, however, only the use of heavy-duty jacks and steel sheeting will get you out without further problems.

If the surface is hard but slippery

- Engage the differential lock ('diff-lock') on the drive axle, if one is fitted. This will reduce any wheel-spin. Remember to switch it off again as soon as you drive onto a better surface
- Drive at a crawling pace in the highest possible gear and with the minimum 'revs'. Try to select a course that avoids you having to turn.

It's against the law to deposit mud on the road to the extent that it could endanger other road users.

## Snow

In falling snow use dipped headlights and slow down. Leave a much greater stopping and separation distance – up to **ten** times the stopping distance on dry roads.

Road markings and traffic signs can be covered by snow. Take extra care at junctions.

High-level or exposed roads are sometimes closed by deep snow. Listen to any weather warnings. Don't try to use such roads if

- Warning signs indicate that the road is closed to large vehicles or other traffic
- Severe weather is forecast

Some country roads in exposed places have marker posts at the side of the road, which tell drivers how deep the snow is. Remember, if a bus gets stuck it could

- Stop snow ploughs from clearing the road
- Delay emergency vehicles
- Cause other road users to become stuck
- Put passengers at risk

## Ploughs and gritting vehicles

Keep out of the way of essential maintenance vehicles. Don't try to overtake a snow plough or gritting vehicle. You may find yourself running into deep snow or skidding on an ungritted stretch of road, which these maintenance vehicles could have treated had you followed on behind them.

Keep well back from gritters. If **they're** out on the road ask yourself whether **you** should be. Their presence could mean that the weather is already bad or that it's expected to be.

## Deep snow

If your vehicle is fitted with a manually selected retarder system or 'diff-lock' engage it before going down a hill covered with snow. Similarly, engage it if your bus gets stuck in deep snow. Remember to switch it off as soon as the vehicle is moving and before making any turn.

Another tactic for freeing a vehicle stuck in snow is to use the highest gear possible to try to get out. Alternating between the reverse and forward gears, if possible, is a good way of getting moving again when the snow is soft. Don't keep revving in a low gear. You'll only make the driving wheels dig in even further.

It's often helpful to keep a couple of strong sacks in your vehicle to put under the drive wheels if you get stuck, but remember the warnings about your vehicle undercarriage. Hardened snow can cause considerable damage. A shovel is often handy if you must go through areas where snow is a problem during the winter.

If you drive on the Continent in the winter make sure that your coach is properly prepared. In some countries you must carry snow chains at certain times of the year. They must be used in bad weather.

Ultimately, ask yourself whether your route should go through an area where such conditions are likely.

**No risk is worth taking.**

## Fog

- Don't drive in dense fog if you can put off the journey
- Avoid driving at all in fog at night
- It's better not to start a journey than to risk driving in fog

If you must drive in fog, **slow down.** Also, keep a safe separation distance from any vehicle in front. If you can see the rear lights of a vehicle in front you're probably too close to stop in an emergency.

A large vehicle travelling in front of you may punch a hole through the fog, making it seem thinner than it really is. Overtaking at that point could quickly lead to a problem. Stay back.

Just because you have a higher seating position doesn't mean that you can see further in fog. Only overtake if you're sure that the road ahead is clear – and then only on a dual carriageway.

Don't speed up if the fog seems to be thin – it could be patchy and you might run into it again. Also, don't speed up if a vehicle comes up close behind you. Keep checking your speedometer to see your true speed. Remember, fog can confuse you and make it difficult to know where you are or how fast you're going.

### Don't take risks.

There aren't many places where you can find a safe place to park a bus in thick fog. You must not leave a bus on or near a road where it could be a danger to other road users. And your passengers won't be pleased with the prospect of spending the night in a lay-by. Certainly don't park a bus anywhere in fog without lights.

### Lights

Use dipped headlights whenever you find it difficult to see. You need to see clearly and be seen at all times.

Use high-intensity rear fog lights and front fog lights (if fitted) when

visibility is less than 100 metres (330 feet). Rear fog lights must be wired so that they only work when the dipped headlights are switched on. Switch off front and rear fog lights when you can see further than 100 metres (330 feet), but beware of patchy fog.

Keep all lights and reflectors clean and make sure that they're working correctly at all times, particularly in bad weather.

### Reflective studs

Reflective studs are provided on dual carriageways and motorways to help drivers to see in poor visibility. The colours of reflective studs are

- **Red** – on the left-hand edge of carriageways
- **White** – to indicate lane markings
- **Amber** – at the right-hand edge of the carriageway and the centre reservation
- **Green** – at slip roads and lay-bys
- **Yellow/Green fluorescent** – at roadwork contraflow systems

On some country roads there are black and white marker posts with red reflectors on the left-hand side and white reflectors on the right-hand side of the road.

All these reflective devices are designed to help you know where you are on the road.

In fog don't

- Drive too close to the centre of the road
- Confuse centre lines with lane markings
- Drive without using headlights
- Speed up because the fog seems to be thin
- Use full beam when following another vehicle. You'll make it more difficult for the other driver to see by casting shadows and causing glare in the mirror

**Slow down and stay back.**

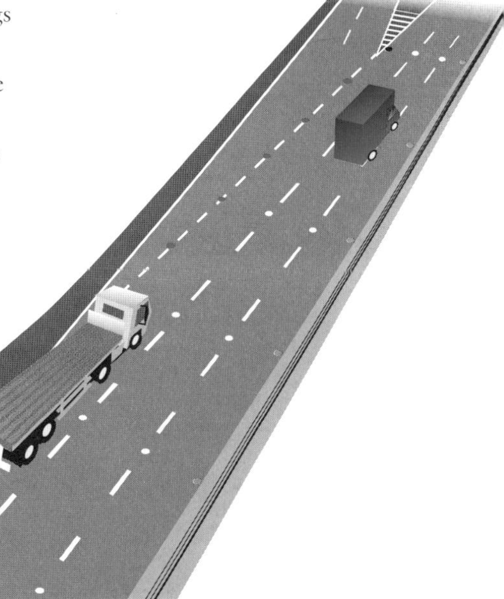

## High winds

In bad weather it's a good idea to listen to, watch or read the weather forecast if you're going to drive

- A double-decker bus or coach
- A high-floor coach
- A light or empty bus, coach or minibus

If you have to drive on roads that often have strong winds such as

- High bridges
- High-level roads
- Exposed viaducts
- Exposed stretches of motorway

listen to advance weather warnings. Ferry crossings will also be affected by very strong winds. There could be delays or cancellations, so it's a good idea to check before setting off.

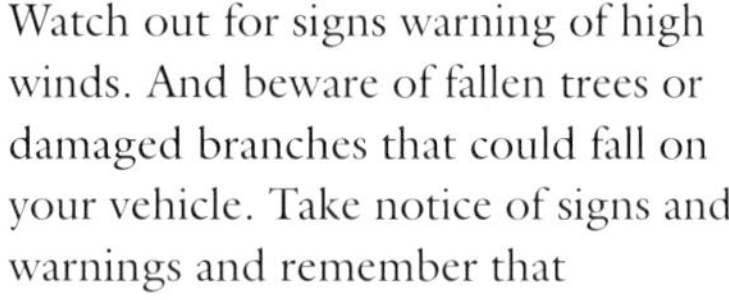

Watch out for signs warning of high winds. And beware of fallen trees or damaged branches that could fall on your vehicle. Take notice of signs and warnings and remember that

- Roads may be closed to certain large vehicles
- There may be delays due to lanes being closed. This is done on high bridges to create empty 'buffer' lanes in the event of any large vehicles being blown off course
- You may need to use another route

If you ignore any signs or warnings you could put your passengers and vehicle at risk. If there's an accident your passengers could be injured and you could be prosecuted and convicted.

**Don't take risks.**

### Other road users

When it's very windy other road users are likely to be affected when

- They overtake you
- You overtake them

Check your mirrors as you overtake to see that they still have control of their vehicle. Also, watch out for vehicles or motorcycles 'wandering' into your lane.

Don't ignore warnings of severe winds. **You can't afford to take risks.**

## Accidents and risk

The word 'accident' is often used incorrectly. An accident is something that happens by chance, or because of unforseen circumstances. But most road traffic accidents are anything **but** accidents. Most happen because drivers make a mistake, fail to see or act on changes in road and traffic conditions, or 'push their luck'.

You should drive at all times with anticipation and awareness. By driving defensively you lessen the risk of an accident.

If, however, you're involved in or have to stop at an accident, you should act decisively and with care to prevent any further damage or injury. Ultimately, your own safety and that of others must be your first concern.

Stay alert. Always try to predict what other road users will do while driving. You also need to understand how your vehicle will affect vulnerable road users such as cyclists, pedestrians and motorcyclists. Pedestrians at the edge of the kerb and cyclists are more vulnerable to being hit by your mirrors or being drawn under your wheels.

Assess every risk and try to eliminate it. You can remove most of the accident risk from your own driving by

- Concentrating
- Staying alert
- Being fully fit
- Observing the changes in traffic conditions
- Planning well ahead
- Driving at a safe speed to suit the road, traffic and weather conditions
- Keeping your vehicle in good overall condition
- Making sure that passengers don't distract you
- Driving safely and sensibly
- Not rushing
- Avoiding the need to act hurriedly

If you're involved in an accident

### You must stop.

It's an offence not to do so.

## At an accident scene

If you're one of the first to arrive at an accident scene your actions could be vital. You must ensure that either you or others

- Warn other traffic by using hazard warning lights, beacons, cones, advance warning triangles, etc.
- Check that there are no naked lights, or take the correct action if there are
- Telephone 999, giving full details of what has happened
- Check that all hazard flashers can be seen. If other road users confuse your signals it could make things worse

### Dealing with injuries

It's best to avoid moving injured people until the emergency services arrive. You should be extremely careful about moving casualties – it could prove fatal. Casualties should only normally be moved if

- They're in need of resuscitation (that is, unconscious)
- In immediate danger (from fire, chemicals, fuel spillage, etc.)

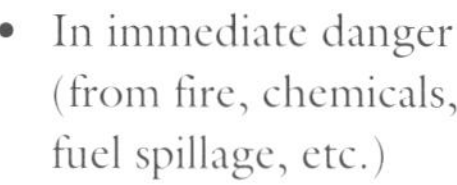

You should

- Move any apparently uninjured people away from the vehicle(s) to a safe place
- Give First Aid if anyone is unconscious
- Check for the effects of shock. A person may appear to be uninjured but might be suffering from shock
- Keep casualties warm but don't give them anything to eat or drink
- Give the **facts** (not assumptions, etc.) to medical staff when they arrive

## Caring for passengers

You must do everything you can to protect your passengers at an accident scene. Decide if there's any further danger and then how best to reduce the risk. Tell passengers what's happening

- Without upsetting them further
- By only giving them accurate information that they need to know

You'll need to decide whether it's appropriate for passengers to

- Stay where they are
- Move to a safer position in the bus, if they're able (e.g., to the front if another vehicle could run into the back)
- Get off the bus carefully and wait in a safe place, which you must select

If you're unable to supervise the movement of your passengers ask someone responsible to do it for you. You must not allow people to wander around. They could put themselves at risk or get in the way of the emergency services.

You should ask for people with medical qualifications to come forward and help.

## On the motorway

Because of the higher speeds on motorways there's more danger of an accident turning into a serious incident. You must inform the motorway police and emergency services as quickly as you can.

- Use the nearest emergency telephone
- Don't cross the carriageway to get to an emergency telephone
- Try to warn oncoming traffic, but don't endanger yourself
- Move any uninjured people well away from the main carriageway and onto an embankment, etc.
- Watch out for emergency vehicles coming along the hard shoulder

### Hazardous materials

If an accident involves a vehicle displaying either a hazard warning information plate or a plain orange rectangle

- Give the emergency services as much information as possible about the labels and any other markings
- Contact the emergency telephone number on the plate of a vehicle involved in any spillage, if a number is given
- Keep well away from such a vehicle unless you have to save a life
- Beware of any liquids, dusts or vapours – no matter how small the amount may appear to be. People have been seriously injured from just a fine spray of corrosive fluid leaking from a pinhole puncture in a tanker

### Documents and information

If your vehicle is involved in an accident you must STOP. It's against the law not to do so. Also, you must

- Inform the police as soon as possible, or in any case within 24 hours, if
  - anybody is injured
  - damage is caused to another vehicle or property and the owner isn't present or can't be found
  - the accident involves any of the animals specified in law
- Produce your insurance documents and driving licence, and give your name and address to any police officer who may require it
- Give these details to any other road user involved in the accident if they have grounds to ask for them

If you can't show your documents at the time, whether anyone is injured or not, you should report the accident to the police as soon as you can, or in any case within 24 hours.

The police may ask you to take your documents to a police station of your choice within seven days (five days in Northern Ireland), or as soon as is reasonably possible if you're already on a journey that takes you out of the country. You must

- Exchange details with any other driver or road user involved in the accident
- Obtain names and addresses of any witnesses who saw the accident

Take notes at the scene so that you have the information when you need it. Make a note of

- The time
- The place
- Street names
- Vehicle registration numbers
- Weather conditions
- Lighting (if applicable)
- Any road signs or road markings

- Road conditions
- Damage to vehicles or property (see p. 55 for the procedure for railway bridge collisions)
- Traffic lights (colour at the time)
- Any indicator signals or warning (horn)
- Any statements made by other people involved
- Any skid marks, debris, etc.

## Fire

Fire can occur on PCVs in a number of locations

- Engine
- Passenger areas
- Kitchens and serveries
- Toilets
- Crew sleeping accommodation
- Luggage lockers
- Transmission
- Tyres
- Fuel system
- Electrical circuits

It's vital that any outbreak is tackled without delay. A vehicle can be destroyed by fire within an alarmingly short period of time.

If you find a fire, or think that there is one, you must act so that danger to others is avoided. It's essential to

- Stop as quickly and safely as possible
- Get everyone off the PCV as quickly as possible. Tell them to stand in a safe place
- Either telephone 999 or get someone else to do it immediately
- Tackle the source with a suitable fire extinguisher, if you can do so safely

If the fire involves a vehicle carrying hazardous materials

- The driver must have been given training to deal with such an emergency. Follow his advice
- The vehicle should carry special fire extinguishers
- Keep the public and other traffic well away from the fire
- Isolate the vehicle, if you can, to reduce danger to the surrounding area
- Make sure that someone calls, immediately, the emergency telephone number given on the hazard warning plate or the load documents
- Warn oncoming traffic

**Stay calm – act quickly.**

## Fire extinguishers

All PCVs should have at least one fire extinguisher. You must know where they're located and how to get them out and use them.

You must know the different types of extinguishers and on which fires they should be used. For example, never tackle a fuel fire with a water 'soda-acid' fire extinguisher. It will only spread the fire.

Most extinguishers smother the source of the fire by using inert gas or a dry powder. Try to isolate the source of the fire. If at all possible

- Disconnect electrical leads
- Cut off the fuel supply

Don't open an engine housing, etc. wide if you can aim the extinguisher through a small gap. Also, avoid operating a fire extinguisher in a confined space.

There are detailed emergency procedures for dealing with vehicles carrying high-risk materials, which must be followed exactly. Leave this to the experts.

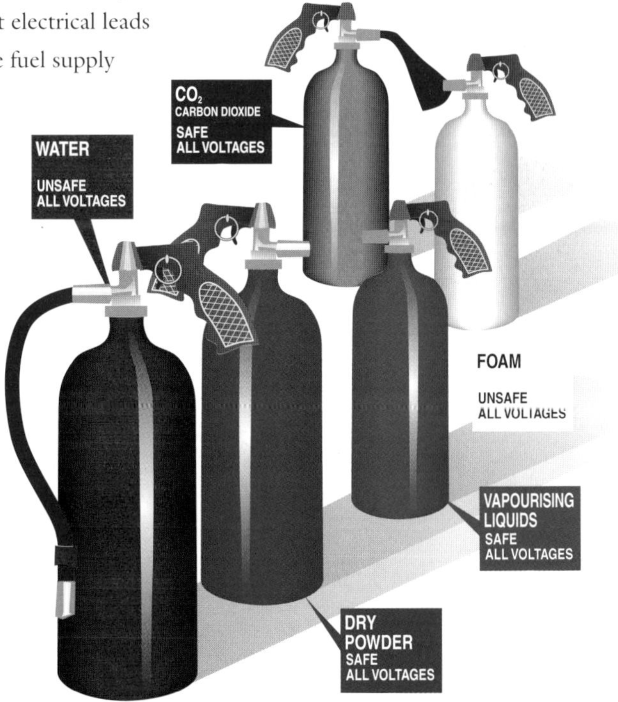

## First Aid

Buses and coaches should carry First Aid equipment. You must know

- Where it is
- How to get at it (if it's kept behind glass or in a safety compartment)
- What's in it
- How and when to use it

As a professional driver, you're encouraged to take some First Aid training. It could help save a life. There are courses available from the

- St John Ambulance Association and Brigade
- St Andrew's Ambulance Association
- British Red Cross Society

The following information may be of general assistance, but there's no substitute for proper training.

### Unconscious victims

It's vital that action is taken within the first three minutes of an incident if a casualty is to be saved. With unconscious victims, gently shake their shoulders and shout 'wake up!' If you get no response remember the letters **A B C**

- **A**irway – must be cleared of any blockage and kept open
- **B**reathing – must be established and maintained
- **C**irculation – must be maintained and severe bleeding stopped

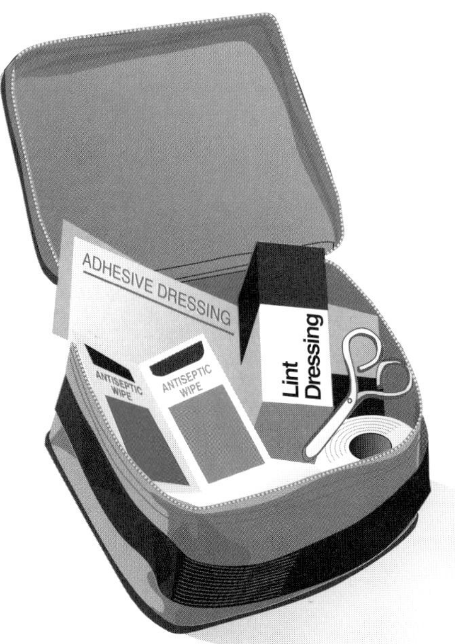

**Breathing stopped** Get breathing started again by

- Removing any blockage such as false teeth, chewing gum, etc.
- Keeping the victim's head tilted backwards to open the airway

Breathing should start and the colour should come back. If not

- Pinch the casualty's nostrils together and blow into the mouth until the chest rises. If the casualty's face is covered in blood use a clean piece of material, such as a handkerchief, to act as a shield
- Let your mouth surround the mouth and nose of small children and babies and blow very gently
- Move your head away and wait for the chest to fall. Listen for breathing or feel for breath against your cheek
- Repeat regularly once every four seconds until the casualty starts to breath again and can carry on breathing without help

**Don't give up!**

Never assume someone is dead. Keep giving mouth-to-mouth resuscitation until medical help comes.

**Breathing unaided** If you suspect a head injury don't move the casualty if at all possible until medical help is available. Only move the casualty if they're in danger of further injury.

Don't try to take off a crash helmet unless it's absolutely essential. You could inflict even more serious injuries on an injured motorcyclist, for example.

If breathing becomes difficult or stops, follow the steps above.
It's vital to obtain skilled medical help as soon as possible. Make sure someone telephones 999.

**Bleeding** To stem the flow of blood put firm pressure on the wound without pressing on anything that may be caught in or sticking out from the wound.

As soon as practicable fasten a pad to the wound with a bandage or length of cloth. Use the cleanest material available.

If a limb is bleeding, but not broken, raise it to reduce the flow of blood. Any restriction of blood circulation for more than a short time could cause long-term injuries.

## Dealing with shock

The effects of shock may not be immediately obvious. Warning signs to look for include

- Rapid pulse
- Pale grey skin
- Sweating
- Rapid shallow breathing

Prompt treatment can help to deal with shock.

- Don't give the casualty anything to eat or drink
- Reassure the victim confidently that they'll be alright. Keep checking them
- Keep any casualties warm and make them as comfortable as you can
- Talk firmly and quietly to anyone who's hysterical
- Don't let shock victims wander into the path of other traffic
- Try not to leave any casualty alone
- Don't move the casualty unless it's necessary
- If a casualty does need to be moved for their own safety, take care to avoid making their injuries worse

## Electric shock

Some accidents involve a vehicle hitting overhead cables or electrical supplies to traffic bollards, traffic lights or street lights. Make a quick check before trying to get someone out of a vehicle in such cases.

Don't touch any person who's obviously in contact with live electricity unless you can use some non-conducting item such as a dry sweeping broom, etc. You must not try to give First Aid until contact has been broken.

## Breakdowns

Many PCV breakdowns involve a tyre bursting, commonly known as a 'blow-out'. These are dangerous because they make a bus difficult to control. They also leave debris on the road, which causes danger to other road users.

### Front wheel blow-outs

A front wheel blow-out can mean that you won't be able to steer the bus properly.

- Keep a tight hold on the steering wheel
- You should always be aware of anything on the left-hand side of your bus
- Signal left
- Try to steer to the left-hand side of the road (or to the hard shoulder on the motorway)
- Slow down gradually – don't brake hard
- Try to stop your bus under control as far to the left as you can
- If you need to, put a warning triangle, cones, etc. behind the vehicle
- Switch on the hazard warning lights if your vehicle's blocking part of the road

If you can avoid braking hard or swerving you should be able to stop the bus without skidding.

### Rear wheel blow-outs

If a rear tyre bursts you might not notice that it's happened. This is because most large vehicles have twin rear wheels. If you carry on driving, the second tyre on that side of the axle could also burst, as it's not designed to run on its own.

A rear wheel blow-out usually has less effect on the steering than a front wheel blow-out. However, the ride will become bumpy. Always try to find out what's causing odd handling.

Follow the same procedure for a front tyre blow-out and pull off the road as safely as possible.

### Safety checks

It's essential to make sure that all wheel nuts are tightened with the approved calibrated torque wrench. The wheel nuts should be checked every day before starting your journey.

# PART FOUR TEST PREPARATION

This part offers details on how to apply and prepare for the practical PCV driving test, together with the officially recommended syllabus. In addition, the individual test requirements are covered.

## The topics covered

- Preparing for the driving test
- Applying for the test
- The official syllabus

The standard required to pass the PCV driving test is high, but then again it should be. After all, you'll be carrying passengers who will be relying on you to deliver them safely to their destinations. Also, the vehicles you'll be licensed to drive require extensive knowledge, skill and responsibility to be driven safely.

The PCV driving test has been carefully designed to assess whether you've reached the required standard. To be properly prepared for the driving test you should cover the specific aspects of the officially recommended syllabus (found on pp. 149–64) and combine this with practice on a wide variety of roads in different traffic conditions. You should be able to demonstrate to the examiner that you can deal with any situation that arises – safely, skilfully and without help or advice.

## Training organisations

There are a number of training organisations concerned with passenger transport, which have established the highest standards of training for the PCV driver. In addition, several large operators have driver-training divisions.

If you wish to work for one of these operators and are accepted onto their scheme you'll be trained to drive using company buses. You may have to pay for this training, or agree to work for the company for a certain time.

The company itself will arrange for your PCV driving test, if you're good enough. Some operators even have examiners of their own who are authorised to conduct tests. Otherwise you'll be tested by a DSA examiner at a PCV driving test centre.

You can find details of a local training group by contacting

- The Confederation of Passenger Transport UK, whose address is at the back of this book
- Your local bus or coach operators
- Your local Training and Enterprise Council (TEC)
- Advertisers in your local press or in trade directories

You'll normally be offered an 'assessment drive', lasting an hour or two. The instructor will then suggest the length of course you'll need and the cost.

Contact more than one training organisation and compare schemes. Try to choose an instructor or organisation with an established reputation for the quality of their instruction and proven PCV test results. Ask what arrangements are made should you need additional training as a result of failing a PCV test. Also, talk to newly qualified PCV drivers about their training.

## Training coverage

It's in your own interest to find out how comprehensive a training course will be before you enrol. The opportunity to drive a variety of vehicles will obviously widen your knowledge and understanding of buses and coaches. In addition, your training should cover driving

- On as many different types of road as possible, including motorways
- In all sorts of driving conditions, including darkness
- On dual carriageways, where the upper speed limit for PCVs applies. (You'll probably be asked to drive on such roads during the PCV test.)

Whether you select operator training, a commercial driver-training school or an individual trainer, with perhaps only one vehicle, it's essential that all aspects of the syllabus set out in this part are covered. You should also have the opportunity to practise the braking and reversing exercises on a suitable off-road site. However, avoid concentrating solely on the off-road exercises.

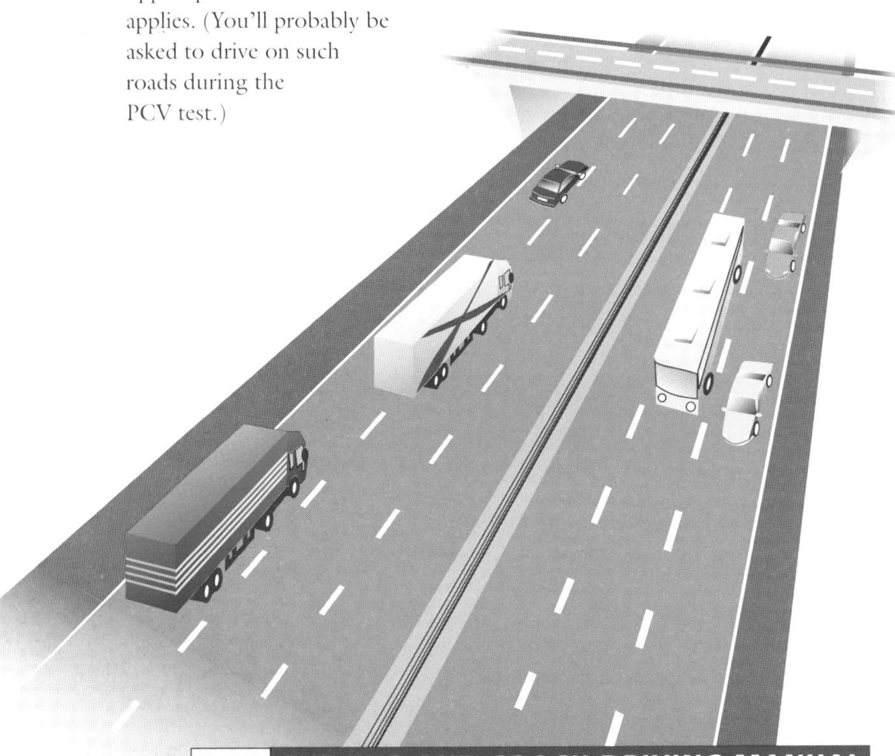

## Causing a nuisance

Creating undue inconvenience for others should be avoided when you practise. Not all road users appreciate the difficulties that a bus driver faces when manoeuvring a large vehicle, especially

- Moving off
- Stopping
- Turning left or right
- In narrow roads

Causing a nuisance to residents and other traffic, or the continuous noise created by

- The hissing of air brakes or revving the engine to build up air pressure
- Persistent stopping and starting

can soon become a reason for complaint in residential areas.

If a local problem exists due to PCV or LGV training already taking place, avoid making the situation worse. Your trainer should be aware of any such difficulties and use an alternative area to practise.

## About the driving test

You should aim for a professional standard when you take the test. You'll pass if the examiner sees that you can

- Drive safely and to a high standard
- Show expert handling of all the controls
- Carry out the set exercises accurately and under control
- Demonstrate a thorough understanding of *The Highway Code* and vehicle safety matters

Examiners are trained to carry out tests to the same high standards nationally. Whether they're DSA or delegated company examiners, all are regularly checked to ensure that your driving will be assessed uniformly. You should have the same result whoever the examiner is and wherever the test takes place. In addition, test routes

- Are as similar as possible
- Include a wide range of typical road and traffic conditions

## The examiner

The examiner will want to see that you drive safely to a high standard under various road and traffic conditions. He or she will

- Give you directions clearly and in good time
- Ask you to carry out set exercises

The examiner will be understanding and sympathetic and will make every effort to allow you to do your best.

Listen carefully to what is said. Examiners appreciate that there may be a higher noise level in some vehicles and so will make sure that you can hear any instructions or directions clearly. If you don't hear or understand something, don't be afraid to say so. The examiner won't mind repeating the instruction.

To avoid distracting you the examiner won't engage in any unnecessary conversation while you're busy driving. However, he or she may talk to you while you aren't driving, just to put you at your ease. Driving examiners are genuinely interested in the people they meet and the work that they do.

## Passengers during the test

A DSA supervising officer (and sometimes other DSA staff) may sit in on your test. However, don't let this worry you. The supervising officer won't be examining you, but making sure that the examiner carries out the test properly. The supervising officer won't interfere with the test or the result, so just carry on as if he or she isn't there.

Your instructor or an accompanying driver is allowed to be present during the test. They must not take any part in it, however.

If you need an interpreter you should arrange for one to come with you on the test. Any interpreter should be someone other than your instructor and at least 16 years old. You should discuss with the examiner (through your interpreter) how you can both ensure that directions or instructions are clearly understood.

Other than those individuals already mentioned above, the regulations don't permit passengers to be carried on a driving test.

## What's covered on the test?

The test will last around 90 minutes. You should drive in the way that your instructor has taught you. If you make a mistake, try not to worry. It may not be serious enough to affect the result of the test. The examiner will be looking for an overall high standard of driving; you're unlikely to fail for one or two minor mistakes.

Apart from general driving, which is described in more detail later in this part, the test will include special exercises, such as

- Reversing within a marked area into a restricted opening
- A braking exercise
- A gear-changing exercise
- Moving off on the level, at an angle, uphill and downhill

Two of the special exercises are carried out on site at the PCV driving test centre. These are the

- Reversing exercise
- Braking exercise

If a delegated company examiner conducts your test they may be carried out on public roads or on an agreed private site.

The examiner will be as helpful as possible and will explain what's required by showing you a diagram of the exercises. You'll then be asked to carry them out. If you're unsure about anything, ask. The examiner will explain again.

During the reversing exercise the examiner will remain outside the vehicle. However, he or she will join you in the vehicle before explaining the braking exercise. The examiner will watch your handling of the controls when you carry out this exercise. Make sure that you understand what's required.

The braking exercise is always carried out before leaving the PCV driving test centre. If your vehicle doesn't pull up satisfactorily the examiner may decide not to continue the test, in the interest of safety.

The remainder of the special exercises will take place during the road section of the test.

## *The Highway Code*

You must know and understand *The Highway Code* thoroughly and put it into practice during the test. Study the latest edition carefully.

Questions on *The Highway Code* also form part of the theory test for drivers of large vehicles. You must pass the theory test before you're permitted to take the practical PCV driving test. However, between 1 January and 30 June 1997 an interim measure will allow the tests to be taken in either order. If the practical driving test is passed first the theory test must be passed within six months. Otherwise a theory test pass certificate is valid for two years.

You may also want to refer to *The Official Theory Test for Large Vehicle Drivers* (The Stationery Office) when you're preparing for the practical test.

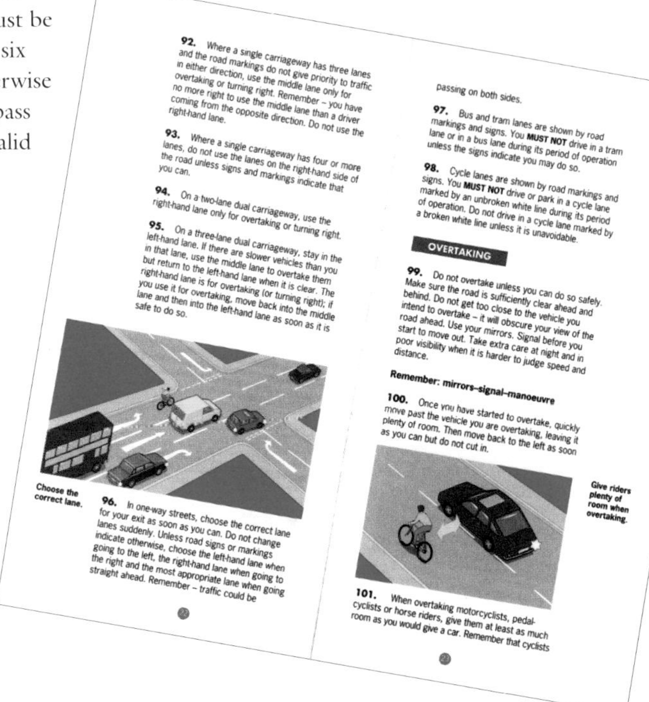

**92.** Where a single carriageway has three lanes and the road markings do not give priority to traffic in either direction, use the middle lane only for overtaking or turning right. Remember – you have no more right to use the middle lane than a driver coming from the opposite direction. Do not use the right-hand lane.

**93.** Where a single carriageway has four or more lanes, do not use the lanes on the right-hand side of the road unless signs and markings indicate that you can.

**94.** On a two-lane dual carriageway, use the right-hand lane only for overtaking or turning right.

**95.** On a three-lane dual carriageway, stay in the left-hand lane. If there are slower vehicles than you in that lane, use the middle lane to overtake them but return to the left-hand lane when it is clear. The right-hand lane is for overtaking (or turning right); if you use it for overtaking, move back into the middle lane and then into the left-hand lane as soon as it is safe to do so.

**Choose the correct lane.**

**96.** In one-way streets, choose the correct lane for your exit as soon as you can. Do not change lanes suddenly. Unless road signs or markings indicate otherwise, choose the left-hand lane when going to the left, the right-hand lane when going to the right and the most appropriate lane when going straight ahead. Remember – traffic could be passing on both sides.

**97.** Bus and tram lanes are shown by road markings and signs. You **MUST NOT** drive in a tram lane or in a bus lane during its period of operation unless the signs indicate you may do so.

**98.** Cycle lanes are shown by road markings and signs. You **MUST NOT** drive or park in a cycle lane marked by an unbroken white line during its period of operation. Do not drive in a cycle lane marked by a broken white line unless it is unavoidable.

**OVERTAKING**

**99.** Do not overtake unless you can do so safely. Make sure the road is sufficiently clear ahead and behind. Do not get too close to the vehicle you intend to overtake – it will obscure your view of the road ahead. Use your mirrors. Signal before you start to move out. Take extra care at night and in poor visibility when it is harder to judge speed and distance.

**Remember: mirrors–signal–manoeuvre**

**100.** Once you have started to overtake, quickly move past the vehicle you are overtaking, leaving it plenty of room. Then move back to the left as soon as you can but do not cut in.

**Give riders plenty of room when overtaking.**

**101.** When overtaking motorcyclists, pedal-cyclists or horse riders, give them at least as much room as you would give a car. Remember that cyclists

## Being fully prepared

When you learned to drive a car it's likely that you waited until you were ready for the driving test before you applied. Driver training for large vehicles is usually intensive, so it may be necessary for either you or your trainer to book your PCV driving test before you've reached the standard required to pass.

Your instructor may offer you a mock test shortly before your real test is due. This will give you an understanding of how the test will be conducted and may alert you to any weaknesses. Make sure that you understand what you're asked to do and, should you need to work on any problem areas, work with your instructor to overcome them.

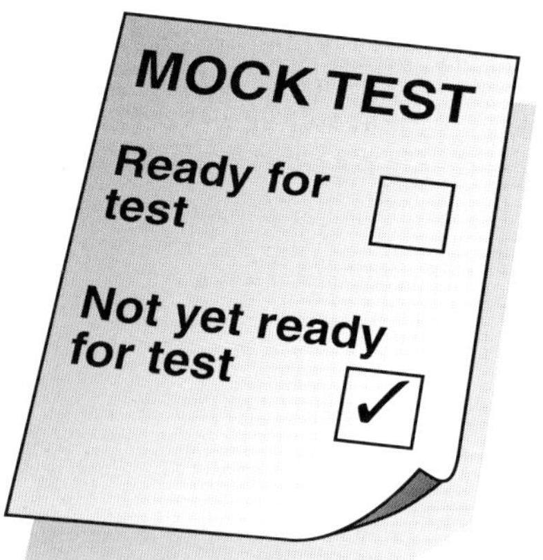

MOCK TEST
Ready for test
Not yet ready for test


Having a test date to aim for is a good incentive. However, drivers acquire skills and understanding at differing rates and it's possible that you may need more time and training than you'd planned. If so, don't be afraid to postpone your test. Be advised by your trainer.

A late cancellation may result in you losing your fee for the driving test, but consider this against driving unaccompanied on your test when you aren't competent. Driving examiners are observers during a driving test – they aren't there to advise you on how to drive. The nature of their work means that they probably won't be in a position to intervene if you make a serious or dangerous mistake.

If your instructor doesn't feel that you have competent, safe control of the vehicle by the time of the test appointment, accept that judgement. You'll be advised about the options for additional training, and an alternative test appointment may be available to you.

Don't take the risk if you aren't fully prepared. Postpone your driving test rather than putting lives at risk.

## The basic requirements

Apply in good time for your practical test, but only when you're sure that your driving has reached the standard set out in this book.

You should ensure that you receive first class instruction and get as much practice as possible. Only when you're driving

- Consistently well
- With confidence
- In complete control
- Without assistance and guidance from your instructor

will you be really ready for your PCV driving test. Those who fail the test often do so because they haven't had enough instruction and practice.

To apply for the test you must have an entitlement to drive PCVs (either a category D provisional licence or a full licence for a category that includes provisional entitlement for the category which you wish to be tested on). In addition, you'll need a valid theory test pass certificate. (Between 1 January and 30 June 1997 the theory test and practical test can be taken in either order.)

## Special circumstances

If you're disabled in any way you'll still take the same PCV driving test as every other candidate. Your examiner may wish to talk to you about your disability and any adaptations fitted to your vehicle. For this reason it's important to give details of your disability when you apply for your test.

To make sure that enough time is allowed for your test it would help DSA to know if

- You're restricted in any way in your movements
- You have any disability that may affect your driving
- You'll need to use an interpreter

Please include this information on your test application form.

If you would like further information please see the list of useful addresses at the back of this book.

## The application form

You can obtain an application form (DLV26) for the driving test from any DSA Area Office (see the list of addresses at the back of this book).

Study the guidance notes carefully, including the table of PCV categories, especially if you wish to drive vehicles in more than one category. Also, you should note that, should you pass the test in a semi- or fully automatic vehicle, you won't be able to drive vehicles with a manual gearbox.

Make sure that you give all the particulars required on the application form, otherwise it will only be returned to you. This will certainly delay your driving test appointment.

Send the correct fee with your application. Posters at test centres list the fees, or your Area Office will tell you. Cheques or postal orders should be crossed and made payable to the Driving Standards Agency. If you send a postal order keep the counterfoil.

**Don't send cash.**

Please read the postal address information carefully and send your application form to the correct address for the appropriate DSA Area Office. Make sure that you

- Address your application correctly – note the post codes
- Enclose the correct fee

Your application will be delayed otherwise.

Send your application to DSA at least 28 days before your preferred date for the test. (In summer, longer notice is often helpful due to the increased demand.) Programmes of tests are arranged well in advance so, if you don't give enough notice, you may not be given your preferred date.

## Booking by credit or debit card

You can book your PCV driving test by telephone using a credit or debit card. If you aren't the card-holder then they should be with you when you make the call.

The following cards are accepted

- Mastercard
- Visa
- Delta

You'll find it helpful to have filled in an application form (DLV26 or DLV26 CC) before making the call. You'll definitely be asked for the information listed on the form. Your appointment date and time will be given to you over the telephone.

The relevant telephone number can be found in the list of DSA Area Offices at the back of this book.

## Trainer booking

DSA now has a facility for trainers to book tests for candidates. Ask at your training school whether you're able to take advantage of the scheme or if you should book the test for yourself.

If you take the test with a delegated examiner from an operator's premises the test will usually be offered to you at the end of the course. The cost will normally be included as part of your agreement with the company, but you may be asked to pay a separate fee.

Trainers wishing to use the trainer booking system should contact their DSA Area Office.

## Saturday and evening tests

Saturday and weekday evening tests are available at some PCV driving test centres. The fees for these are higher than for a test during normal working hours on weekdays. You can get details from

- DSA Area Offices
- PCV driving test centres
- Your instructor

## Your test appointment

When your application has been received by the DSA Area Office you'll be sent notification of the date, time and place of your appointment. This also acts as a receipt of your fee. If you don't receive notification after 21 days, contact the DSA Area Office as soon as possible.

Check your appointment notification as soon as you receive it to make sure that the date and time of the test appointment are suitable. If you can't keep the appointment you should notify the DSA Area Office immediately and return your appointment notification.

To cancel, you must give at least five clear (working) days' notice. That means five whole working days – not counting the day the DSA Area Office receives your notification nor the day of your test. If you don't give enough notice you'll forfeit your fee and will have to re-apply with another fee.

### Change of address or vehicle

Please notify the DSA Area Office immediately if you change your address before the day of your appointment. Also, you'll need to inform them if you have to bring a different vehicle from the one described on your application form. Otherwise, there could be delay when you arrive for your test.

Inform the driving examiner at the test centre, either beforehand or as soon as you arrive, if there's any last-minute change of vehicle.

## Extended tests

If you're found guilty of certain driving offences the courts may direct you to retake your PCV driving test. And for some offences, which involve disqualification from driving for a period of time, you may need to take an extended car driving test. This means that

- It will be necessary to apply to the DVLA for a provisional licence entitlement
- You may only apply for a PCV test after passing an extended category B driving test
- You'll have to pass a normal PCV driving test if you previously held a PCV entitlement and wish to regain it

There are higher fees for extended car driving tests, but not for the associated PCV driving test.

Remember, if you lose your category B (car) entitlement you'll lose your PCV entitlement. Your PCV entitlement may be returned on passing the category B test, but this is at the discretion of the Secretary of State for Transport.

This syllabus lists the skills and knowledge required to be a good bus or coach driver and to pass the PCV practical driving test. Use the syllabus as a check-list while training.

Make sure that you understand all the areas covered. Other parts of this book explain in more detail the various topics in the syllabus. For some specialist information you'll need to refer to other sources. Your local library should be able to help. You can also ask your instructor for advice.

During your driving test you won't be tested on all the items listed in the syllabus. However, you do need to understand them all. You need to know about **all** the aspects of being a safe and professional driver. While you're driving your examiner will watch that you put your knowledge into practice. Think of passing the test as only one stage in becoming a good driver.

If you drive a PCV for which no special driving test is needed, this syllabus will help you to achieve the high standard of driving required for your own safety and that of your passengers.

## Knowledge

You must have a thorough knowledge and understanding of

**1.** The latest edition of *The Highway Code*, especially those sections that concern buses

**2.** Regulations governing drivers' permitted hours (EC 3820/1985)

**3.** Regulations relating to the carriage of passengers (Public Passenger Vehicles Act 1981 and 1990 amendments)*

**4.** General motoring regulations, especially

- road traffic offences
- holding and producing driving licences
- holding an operator's and road fund licences, and displaying discs where applicable
- holding and displaying community bus permits, where applicable
- insurance requirements (including 'green cards' or bail bonds that may be needed when abroad)
- the Temp 100 regulations, if you intend to drive outside the UK
- the information required to be shown on PCV manufacturers' plates
- annual testing and the certification requirements for tachographs and speed limiters
- the importance of regular vehicle maintenance and defect reporting procedures

**5.** Health and Safety legislation, as it applies to PCV duties

You must also have a basic understanding of the function of the component parts of a PCV, including

**6.** Internal combustion engines

- petrol
- diesel
- other fuels

**7.** Power and control units in electrically propelled vehicles, if appropriate

**8.** Ancillary and control systems

**9.** The body and its equipment

*Note: Certain minibuses, mobile project buses, playbuses, historic vehicles and community buses are subject to a relaxation of the Public Service and Passenger Carrying Vehicle regulations. If you drive one of these vehicles you must be aware of any restrictions on its use.

If your vehicle is equipped with a trailer, you must know which legal requirements apply.

## Legal requirements

To learn to drive a PCV you must

**1.** Be 21 years old*

**2.** Meet the stringent eyesight requirements

**3.** Be medically fit to drive PCVs of any type

**4.** Hold a full car licence (category B or, if issued prior to 1990, group A)

**5.** Hold and comply with the conditions for holding either

- a provisional PCV category D entitlement or
- a full PCV entitlement for another category of vehicle, which confers provisional entitlement for the vehicle you wish to drive

**6.** Be sure that any vehicle driven

- is legally roadworthy
- has the required manufacturer's plate
- has a current test certificate that covers its use
- is properly licensed and has the correct tax disc displayed (and 'O' licence or permit disc, if required)
- complies with the requirements of the tachograph and speed limiter legislation and displays the required certificates, if applicable
- meets minimum vehicle requirements if used for a PCV driving test

**7.** Make sure that the vehicle being driven is properly insured for its use, especially if it's on contract hire

**8.** Display L plates to the front and rear of the vehicle (D plates, if you wish, when driving in Wales)

**9.** Be accompanied by a supervisor who holds a valid full UK licence for the category of vehicle being driven

**10.** Be aware of the legal requirement to notify the DVLA of any medical condition that could affect safe driving

**11.** Ensure that all information required on the vehicle by law (referred to as the 'legal lettering') is displayed, as applicable

- seating/standing capacity
- emergency exit location
- fuel cut-off switch
- electrical isolator switch

*Note: You may learn to drive a PCV and take the driving test between the ages of 18 and 21, but if you pass you aren't permitted to carry passengers unless the vehicle is covered by a Public Service Vehicle operator's licence, a bus or community bus permit, and either

- The bus has no more than 16 passenger seats and you drive only in the UK or
- The route mileage doesn't exceed 50 km (31 miles)

- First Aid equipment
- fire extinguisher(s)
- unladen weight of vehicle
- height, displayed in the cab if the vehicle is over 3.66 metres (12 feet)
- registered company name and address
- engine stop button

You must also avoid

**12.** Using any mobile telephone or radio transmitter whilst driving the vehicle (except for limited use of Band III radio systems used for route control and emergency purposes)

**13.** Stopping on the hard shoulder of a motorway to use any mobile telephone or radio transmitter (unless in an emergency)

**14.** Using any public address system fitted in the vehicle to give any commentary whilst driving (except for brief location information which may be given using a 'hands off' system)

**15.** Driving the vehicle whilst

- issuing tickets
- giving change
- holding a conversation, other than in an emergency
- being distracted
- smoking
- passenger doors are open

**16.** In addition, you must know and apply the legal requirements relating to the vehicle and its use, where applicable, in respect of

- speed limits
- seating/standing capacity
- fire extinguishers
- First Aid equipment (location and use)
- interior lighting during the hours of darkness
- the carriage and consumption of alcoholic drinks
- the emptying of toilet waste storage tanks
- hazardous substances that may be brought on board by passengers

## Vehicle controls, equipment and components

You must

**1.** Understand the function and use of the main controls of the vehicle

- accelerator
- clutch, if applicable
- gears
- footbrake
- handbrake
- steering, including power-assisted steering

and be able to use them competently

**2.** Know the effects speed limiters will have on the control of your vehicle, especially when you intend to overtake

**3.** Know the principles of the various systems of retarders that may be fitted to PCVs
- electric
- engine-driven
- exhaust brakes

and when they should be brought into operation

**4.** Know the function of all other controls and switches on the vehicle and be able to use them competently

**5.** Understand the information given by
- gauges
- warning lights or buzzers
- other displays on the instrument panel

**6.** Be familiar with the operation of tachographs and their charts and any other time, speed or distance recording equipment that may be fitted. You should know what action to take if a fault develops in this equipment

**7.** Know which checks should be made before starting a journey

**8.** Know the safety factors relating to
- seated and standing passengers
- loading
- stability
- controls of any driver-operated doors
- stowing luggage when passengers are carried

**9.** Be able to carry out routine safety checks and identify defects, especially with the
- engine
  - performance
  - fuel systems
  - lubricating systems and oil levels
  - coolant temperature and levels
  - exhaust systems
- gearbox
  - operation
  - controls
- transmission
- braking system
  - efficiency
  - operation
- steering (including power-assisted systems)
- suspension
- tyres and wheel security
- heating, air conditioning and ventilation
- electrical systems, including
  - lights
  - destination displays

  - wipers and washers
  - bells, buzzers and linked 'bus stopping' displays
  - emergency 'exit insecure' warning devices, if fitted
  - horns
  - fuses, cut-outs and relays

- exterior bodywork
  - panels
  - fittings
  - trim
  - access doors
  - rear view mirrors

- interior bodywork
  - seating
  - fittings
  - trim
  - floor coverings
  - mirrors

and, where fitted,

- seat belts and grab rails
- equipment for wheelchair access and security
- mechanically, electrically or air-operated doors
- adjustable suspension on 'kneeling' vehicles
- securing devices on emergency doors
- equipment for breaking emergency windows
- staircases

## Road user behaviour

You must know how to limit the risk of being involved in a road traffic accident by understanding

**1.** The most common causes of those accidents

**2.** Which road users are more vulnerable, for example

- children
- young riders and drivers
- elderly drivers
- elderly or infirm pedestrians
- cyclists and motorcyclists
- learner drivers

**3.** The rules, risks and effects of drinking before driving

**4.** The effects on your performance of

- illnesses
- drugs
- cold remedies
- other medication
- tiredness

**5.** The importance of complying with rest period regulations

**6.** How to

- concentrate
- plan ahead
- anticipate the actions of other road users

## Vehicle characteristics

You must know

**1.** The most important principles concerning braking distances under various road, weather and loading conditions

**2.** The different handling characteristics of vehicles with regard to

- speed
- stability
- braking
- manoeuvrability
- turning circles

**3.** That some other vehicles, such as cycles and motorcycles, are less easily seen than others

You must also be aware of

**4.** Blind spots that occur on many large vehicles

**5.** The need to be extra vigilant when reversing any PCV into or out of a bay at boarding points or in workshops

**6.** The safe angle of tilt, which must not be exceeded when driving high vehicles

**7.** The risks and difficulties presented when

- long vehicles negotiate speed reduction humps or humpback bridges
- high vehicles are driven along roads with an adverse camber, thus leading to possible collisions with
  - shop blinds
  - buildings
  - road signs
  - traffic lights
  - telephone poles
  - overhead cables
  - trees
  - lamp standards
  - scaffolding
  - other high vehicles
- vehicles with large mirrors pass close to pedestrians, street 'furniture' or other vehicles
- heavy vehicles drive on, or close to, soft or damaged verges
- the vehicle being driven encounters the minimum clearance needed under bridges

**8.** The difficulties caused by the characteristics of both your own and other vehicles, and be able to take the appropriate action to reduce any risks that may arise

Examples of situations requiring special care are when

- long wheel-base coaches, buses and large goods vehicles move to the right before making a sharp left turn
- articulated vehicles take an unusual line before negotiating corners, roundabouts or entrances
- short wheel-base vehicles with front and rear overhang turn left or

right, or when at bus stops, lay-bys, pedestrian crossings, etc.

- cycles, motorcycles and high-sided vehicles are buffeted in strong winds, especially on exposed sections of road
- turbulence created by coaches, double-decker buses and large goods vehicles travelling at speed affect
  - pedestrians
  - cyclists
  - motorcyclists
  - vehicles towing caravans
  - smaller vehicles

## Road and weather conditions

You must

**1.** Know about the hazards that can arise when driving on various types of road with differing volumes of traffic, such as

- country lanes
- single-track roads
- one-way streets
- those with bus lanes
- contraflow systems
- those in built-up areas
- three-lane roads
- dual carriageways with various speed limits
- trunk roads with two-way traffic
- motorways
- roads or reserved areas where light rapid transit vehicles (LRTs or 'supertrams') operate
- busways

**2.** Know about the hazards that can arise when driving in various weather conditions, such as

- strong sunlight
- rain
- snow and ice
- fog
- wind, especially when driving high vehicles

and at all times of the day and night

**3.** Know which surfaces will provide better or poorer grip when accelerating and braking

**4.** Drive sensibly and anticipate how the conditions may affect the driving of other road users

**5.** Understand the need to be aware of other road users when pulling up at bus stops, especially near junctions

**6.** Appreciate the need to give correct signals, especially before pulling up at

- bus stops
- road junctions
- pedestrian crossings, etc.

**7.** Recognise the special risks when passengers board or alight from your vehicle, such as

- schoolchildren
- elderly people
- the disabled
- those with
  - babies
  - toddlers
  - pushchairs
  - luggage

**8.** Be aware of the presence of other road users by making effective use of the mirrors and by looking round before moving off from a standstill. Watch out, in particular, for the passenger who attempts to board or alight as you move off

## Traffic signs, rules and regulations

You must

**1.** Have a thorough knowledge and understanding of the meanings of traffic signs and road markings, especially those relating to

- bus lanes, which may also permit cycles and taxis
- bus priority systems
- light rapid transit systems

**2.** Be able to recognise and comply with traffic signs that point out

- weight limits
- height limits
- length limits
- width limits
- prohibited entry for motor vehicles
- no left or right turns
- loading/unloading restrictions
- roads designated Red Routes
- traffic calming measures

**Note:** Some signs may exempt buses.

## Vehicle control and road procedure

You must have the knowledge and skill to take the following precautions, some of which will require assistance.

**1.** Before getting into the vehicle check that

- you have all the required paper-work (especially for foreign trips)
- all required discs and certificates are displayed
- there are no obstructions round your vehicle
- the emergency exit(s) operate correctly and are closed securely
- all bulbs, lenses and reflectors are fitted, clean and undamaged
- all lights, including indicators and stop lights, are undamaged and working
- tyres and wheel nuts are free from obvious defects (visual check)
- all windows and mirrors are clean and free of traffic grime and cracks

- all body panels are secure
- all external lockers and crew compartment doors are secure
- there are no fluid or air system leaks
- fuel and electrical isolation switches are clearly marked and turned on
- all route numbers and destination blinds or displays are correct (or replaced by information that indicates that the vehicle isn't in service)*

**2.** After entering the vehicle check

- the correct operation of any warning device fitted to an emergency exit that isn't visible from the driving position
- that the entrance and exit doors (if fitted) operate correctly, and that any warning systems work properly
- the location of the fire extinguisher(s) and First Aid equipment
- that heating, air conditioning or ventilation equipment is working properly and set for the conditions
- that the bell or buzzer signal and any passenger information system works
- that all gangways and staircases are clean, clear and free from defects
- that all seats are clean, secure and free from defects
- that the interior lighting operates correctly, including the exit/ entrance step lights
- that equipment for wheelchair access is operational

where these items are fitted, and

- that any graffiti is removed at the earliest opportunity, especially if it might cause offence
- that any luggage or equipment is safely stowed

**3.** Before starting the engine check

- that the handbrake is applied and the gear selector is in neutral or the 'start' position
- your seat, if necessary, for
  - height
  - distance from the controls
  - support and comfort
  - maximum vision
- the mirrors, if necessary, to give a clear view of
  - traffic behind
  - the entrance/exit
  - intending passengers
  - the upper deck, where appropriate
- the doors (if fitted) are closed
- seat belts (if fitted) are in use

*Note: Controls for route and destination displays are usually on board the vehicle. Adjust them as necessary.

**4.** When you start the engine, but before moving off, check that

- the vehicle lights are on, if required
- gauges indicate correct pressures for braking and ancillary systems
- no warning lights are showing, which indicate it's unsafe to drive the vehicle
- no warning buzzer is operating
- all fuel and temperature gauges are operating normally and that there's sufficient fuel for your journey
- suspension systems are at the correct height, if appropriate
- all doors are closed
- all equipment operates correctly (wipers, washers, indicators, etc.)
- special access facilities, such as kneeling suspension, ramps or lifts, are correctly adjusted or stowed
- it's safe, by looking all round. Before moving off especially check
  - the blind spots
  - entry/exit door(s) or boarding platform(s)
  - near the wheels

**Note:** Air-operated systems, such as suspension and doors, may come into operation as air pressure builds up. Ensure this happens safely.

**5.** At the first opportunity, and **before** carrying passengers, check the brakes and steering for correct and effective operation. Also check that exhaust emissions aren't excessive (when the engine's warm)

**6.** When driving you must be able to

- move off safely
  - straight ahead
  - at an angle
  - on the level
  - uphill
  - downhill
- select the correct road position and appropriate gear at all times
- take effective observation in all traffic conditions and give appropriate signals, when necessary
- drive at a speed appropriate to the road, traffic and weather conditions
- anticipate changes in traffic conditions
- take the correct action at all times and exercise care in the use of the controls
- move into the appropriate traffic lane correctly and in good time
- pass stationary vehicles safely
- meet, overtake and cross the path of other vehicles safely
- turn right or left, or drive ahead at junctions, crossroads or roundabouts
- keep a safe separation gap when following other vehicles
- act correctly at all types of pedestrian crossing
- show proper regard for the safety of all other road users, particularly the most vulnerable

- keep up with the flow of traffic where it's safe and appropriate to do so, whilst observing all speed limits
- comply with
  - traffic regulations
  - traffic signs
  - signals given by authorised persons, police officers, traffic wardens or school crossing patrols
- take the correct action on signals given by other road users
- stop the vehicle safely at all times
- show courtesy and consideration to passengers at all times, particularly those with special needs
- wait until elderly or disabled passengers are seated
- be aware at all times of the effects that harsh braking, acceleration or steering will have on passengers, especially those
  - standing
  - moving toward exits
  - moving away from entrances

  Pay particular attention to the care of
  - the elderly
  - the disabled
  - mothers with babies or toddlers
- cross safely all types of level crossings, such as railway or light rapid or railed transit systems (LRTs or 'supertrams')
- select safe and suitable places to stop the vehicle close to the nearside kerb, as is practicable, when requested
  - on the level
  - facing uphill
  - facing downhill
  - before reaching a parked vehicle
- leave sufficient room to move away when the platform of the vehicle's close to passenger boarding points at bus stops and when requested on 'hail and ride' services
- stop the vehicle in an emergency
  - safely
  - as quickly as possible
  - under full control
  - within a reasonable distance
- reverse the vehicle
  - under control
  - with effective observation
  - accurately
- enter a restricted opening to the left or right, and stop with the extreme rear of the vehicle where required (when carrying out a reversing exercise with a delegated examiner)
- follow advertised timetables and, in particular, not depart early from published timing points

**7.** You must be able to carry out, as necessary, all these checks and manoeuvres
- safely and expertly

- in daylight
- during the hours of darkness

Where your actions may affect other road users you must

- make proper use of the mirrors
- take effective observation
- give signals, when necessary
- act predictably

For the PCV driving test you'll be asked to carry out specific exercises to demonstrate your ability to stop quickly and to reverse. If the test isn't conducted by a DSA examiner but by a delegated (company) examiner these manoeuvres may be carried out on the public roads.

**8.** Before leaving the driver's position you must make sure that

- the vehicle is stopped in a safe, legal and secure place
- the handbrake is on
- the gear lever/selector is in neutral or 'park'
- the engine is stopped
- the keys have been removed from the starter switch, if applicable
- the electrical system is switched off, unless lights or other systems are required. (On some vehicles the switch may not be within reach of the driving position.)
- you won't endanger anyone when you open any door

**9.** When leaving a vehicle make sure that

- all windows are closed
- the passenger door is secure (if fitted)
- you take all possible precautions to prevent theft of the vehicle
- any available anti-theft device is used (e.g., immobilizer/alarm)
- you've selected a safe place to leave the unattended vehicle
- the parking place is
  - legal (not a 'no waiting' zone)
  - safe (it won't cause any danger to others)
  - convenient (not blocking any access or exit)
  - suitable (level and firm enough to support the weight of the vehicle)

**10.** If you'll be leaving the vehicle but the public will still have access (for instance, on playbuses or mobile project vehicles) ensure that

- the cab area is isolated
- a responsible person is in attendance

## Additional knowledge

You must know

**1.** The importance of inspecting all tyres on the vehicle for

- correct pressure
- signs of wear
- evidence of damage
- safe tread depth
- objects between twin tyres

– indications of overheating

**2.** Safe driving principles that will help to prevent skids occurring, and the action to take if they do occur

**3.** How to drive when the road is

– icy or snow-covered

– flooded

– covered by excess surface water, loose chippings or spillages

**4.** What to do if you're involved in a road traffic accident

– that results in either injury, damage or fire

– where there's a spillage of hazardous material

– where danger to other road users results from an obstruction caused by an immobilized vehicle

– on a motorway

**5.** The action to take if your vehicle breaks down during the day time or at night on a

– bend

– road with two-way traffic

– busy dual carriageway

– clearway

– motorway

– railway or LRT crossing

with particular reference to the safety of passengers

**6.** The correct procedure to adopt if an accident occurs that involves a passenger either travelling on your vehicle (e.g., falling over, etc.) or boarding or alighting

**7.** The dimensions of your vehicle, including the correct height (especially that of double-decker vehicles, in respect to dangers presented by low bridges, etc.)

**8.** The weight of your vehicle, in respect to restrictions on weak bridges, etc.

**9.** The correct procedure to adopt if it becomes necessary to reverse the vehicle while carrying passengers

**10.** The differences between toughened and laminated glass used in windows and windscreens

**11.** How to use the hammer or similar tool to exit from the vehicle in an emergency

**12.** Basic First Aid for use on the road

**13.** The correct legal procedure (defined in the 1990 amendments to the 1981 PSV regulations) to be adopted by the driver or, where present, a conductor or courier, in respect to any passenger(s) whose behaviour or condition affects the

– safety of other passengers

– comfort of other passengers

– safety of the crew

**14.** The appropriate action to take when handed or when finding

– any lost property

– suspicious packages

**15.** The correct action to take in the event of a passenger, or intending passenger, attempting to alight from or board a moving vehicle

**16.** How and when to use fire extinguishers fitted to the vehicle

**17.** How to evacuate a PCV when necessary

**18.** How and when to use emergency radio and public address systems, if fitted

You must appreciate

**19.** The importance of avoiding any action that could cause offence or provoke physical retaliation

**20.** The need to keep control of the permitted number of standing passengers – especially at peak travel times

**21.** The need to use safe driving techniques and to obey all speed limits when attempting to maintain schedules laid down in the operator's timetable

**22.** The principles of passenger care, including how to

– communicate effectively

– assist passengers with special needs

– help passengers unfamiliar with the service

**23.** The importance of presenting a positive image of your company and the industry through your appearance and conduct and the condition of your vehicle

You must be able to

**24.** Make a written report, promptly, detailing any defects or symptoms of defects that could adversely affect the safe operation of vehicles. You should submit it to the designated person. (The recommended system requires a daily 'nil' return to be made to ensure that checks are made.)

**25.** Appreciate when defects are serious enough to require an unroadworthy vehicle to be removed from service

**26.** Judge whether a defect is serious enough to cause a vehicle to be unsafe to be driven at all

## Motorway driving

You must have a thorough practical knowledge of the special

- Rules
- Regulations
- Driving techniques

that apply to motorways. In particular, you should know about

- Overtaking
- Exercising lane discipline
- Lanes that are prohibited to certain PCVs
- When speed limiters affect driving
- Where PCV speed limits differ to those applying to other traffic
- Where temporary speed limits apply when joining and leaving motorways
- Breakdowns and emergencies
- Driving in all weather conditions
- The principal causes of accidents on motorways

## Safe working practices

You should

**1.** Know the risks involved in jumping down from cabs (where applicable) and avoid them

**2.** Ensure that all doors are closed before the vehicle is moved

**3.** Follow safety guidelines when operating

- under
  - raised engine cowlings
  - raised luggage compartment hatches
  - overhead cables
  - any vehicle
- near
  - inspection pits
  - wheelchair lift controls
  - refuelling points
  - parked vehicles (especially those likely to be moved or with air suspension)
- whilst
  - carrying out roadside repairs
  - inflating tyres
  - near any vehicle supported on jacks
  - refuelling
  - topping up oil or water

**4.** Wear protective clothing, including gloves, when

- refuelling
- topping up oil or water
- checking battery levels
- emptying waste systems

**5.** Know where company policy permits the driver to carry out minor repairs, but do so only

- if you fully understand how to locate the fault and are able to put it right properly
- if you can do so without endangering yourself or others
- with the aid of appropriate equipment, if it's needed
- if you're sure that any work you do won't invalidate any manufacturer's warranty

If in doubt, refer to your company.

## Revised legislation

Buses carrying children must display a distinctive yellow reflective sign on the front and rear, unless running a scheduled service for use by the general public. Buses displaying the sign are permitted to use hazard warning lights when stationary and when children are boarding or alighting.

From February 1998

- All minibuses
- All coaches

will be required to have seat belts fitted if they're used for the carriage of three or more children.

The '3 for 2' concession, which allowed three children under 14 years to sit in seats fitted with two seat belts, has been discontinued. When seat belts are fitted they should be worn.

This part looks at what the practical driving test requires of the driver.

## The topics covered

- What to expect on the day
- The reversing exercise
- The braking exercise
- The vehicle controls
- Other controls
- Moving off
- The gear-changing exercise
- Using the mirrors
- Giving signals
- Acting on signs and signals
- Making progress
- Controlling your speed
- Separation distance
- Awareness and anticipation
- Hazards
- Selecting a safe place to stop
- Uncoupling and recoupling
- *The Highway Code*
- The test results

## Attending the test

PCV driving tests are conducted to a strict timetable. Make sure that you arrive in good time, otherwise your test may not go ahead and you'll lose your fee.

The test will last about 90 minutes, so make sure that you won't exceed the number of hours that you're allowed to drive by law, and that you have sufficient fuel.

When you meet the examiner you'll be asked to sign a declaration that the vehicle you're using for the test is fully insured for that purpose. Make sure that you're properly insured for any hired vehicle you use.

### Your licence

You should bring

- Your full car licence (category B)
- The appropriate PCV licence entitlement
  - provisional or
  - full PCV for a category that gives you provisional entitlement

  It's your responsibility to ensure that you have the appropriate licence entitlement
- Theory test pass certificate, if appropriate

If you don't have your valid, signed driving licence(s) with you the examiner may not be able to conduct your test.

### Photographic identification

You'll need to take with you a form of photographic identification. The following are acceptable

- A current signed passport. This doesn't have to be a British one
- Any of the following identification cards, provided they have your photograph **and** your signature
  - workplace identity card
  - trade union or students' union membership card
  - a card for the purchase of rail tickets
  - cheque guarantee or credit card with photo insert
- A photograph of yourself that's been confirmed by an acceptable person as being a true likeness of you

Your test may be cancelled if you can't provide one of these.

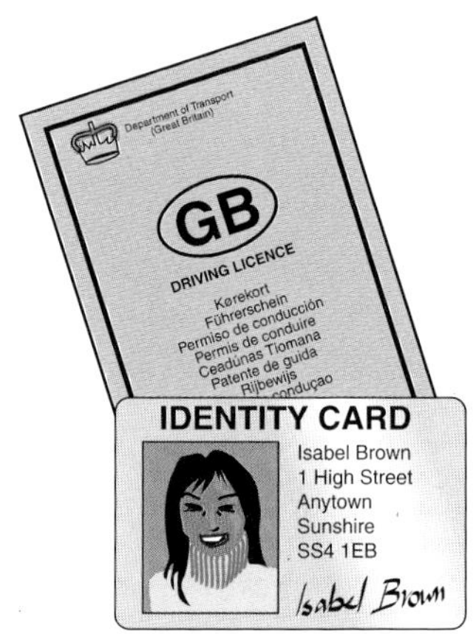

## Preparing your vehicle

To avoid wasting your own time and the examiner's, make sure that your test vehicle

- Has no passengers
- Is in the category in which you wish to hold a licence
- Doesn't exceed 18.28 metres (60 feet) in length
- Has L plates visible to the front and rear (D plates, if you wish, in Wales)
- Isn't being used on a trade licence or displaying trade registration plates
- Has a secure seat for the examiner, from which he or she can observe the driver

It would be unusual for you or your vehicle not to meet the above requirements, but where vehicles have been adapted for other purposes they may not be suitable for the purposes of the test. If you're in doubt, ask DSA.

Make sure that your vehicle has enough fuel, not only for the test (at least 20 miles) but also for you to return to base.

You'll be asked to carry out a gear-changing exercise during the test, unless your vehicle's fitted with automatic transmission. Some modern vehicles with automated and semi-automatic gear-shifting systems may not be suitable for a manual test.

The driver taking a manual test must be able to select the gears requested by the examiner and is required to use a clutch pedal whilst moving off, stopping and changing gear.

### Safety checks

Make sure that your vehicle is in a thoroughly roadworthy condition, especially

- Stop lamps
- Direction indicators
- Lenses/reflectors
- Mirrors
- Brakes
- Tyres
- Exhaust/silencer
- Windscreen/washer/wipers

## What's being tested?

To drive a bus, coach and some midibuses and minibuses unaccompanied you must first pass the PCV driving test. It lasts about 90 minutes, and during this time you'll be expected to drive in an expert and professional manner. The DSA examiner will carry out the special exercises at the driving test centre. The delegated company examiner may carry out the special exercises on a quiet public road or on an off-road private site.

The special exercises include

- A reversing exercise
- A braking exercise
- The uncoupling and recoupling exercise, where applicable

On the road, the drive will include a gear-changing exercise and the route will cover a wide variety of road and traffic conditions. The route will take in roads carrying two-way traffic, dual carriageways and, where possible, one-way systems.

You'll be expected to demonstrate that you can move off smoothly and safely both uphill and downhill, in addition to moving off normally ahead and at an angle.

You'll also need to show that you can safely

- Meet other vehicles
- Overtake
- Cross the path of other vehicles
- Keep a safe separation distance
- Negotiate various types of roundabouts
- Exercise correct lane discipline
- Display courtesy and consideration to other road users especially
  - pedestrians
  - riders on horseback
  - cyclists
  - motorcyclists
- Apply the correct procedure at
  - pedestrian crossings
  - level crossings (both railway and tramway, where appropriate)
  - traffic signals
  - road junctions

You'll need to show

- Effective use of the mirrors
- Correct use of signals
- Alertness and anticipation
- Correct use of speed
- Observance of speed limits
- Expert use of the controls

At the end of your test you'll be asked questions on vehicle safety.

## Preliminaries

The examiner won't conduct an eyesight test at the start of your test because you'll need to have already met the eyesight and medical requirements before your PCV provisional entitlement was granted.

### Before you start the engine

The examiner expects that you've checked and prepared your bus for driving and for taking the test. You aren't expected to carry out a time-consuming or extensive check when he or she is with you. However, before you start your engine you must always be sure that

- All doors are properly closed
- Your seat is correctly adjusted and comfortable so that you
  - can reach all the controls easily
  - have good all-round vision
- Your driving mirrors are correctly adjusted
- Your seat belt is fastened, correctly adjusted and comfortable, if fitted
- The handbrake is on
- The gear lever is in neutral

It's best to develop good habits and to practise this routine while you're learning. The examiner won't be impressed if you have to make adjustments during the test that should have been carried out before it began.

### After you start the engine

Don't attempt to drive a vehicle fitted with air brakes until the gauges show the correct pressure or when any warning device (a buzzer sounding or a light flashing) is operating.

If you're driving a vehicle with automatic transmission you should make sure that the safety checks which apply to your vehicle have been carried out.

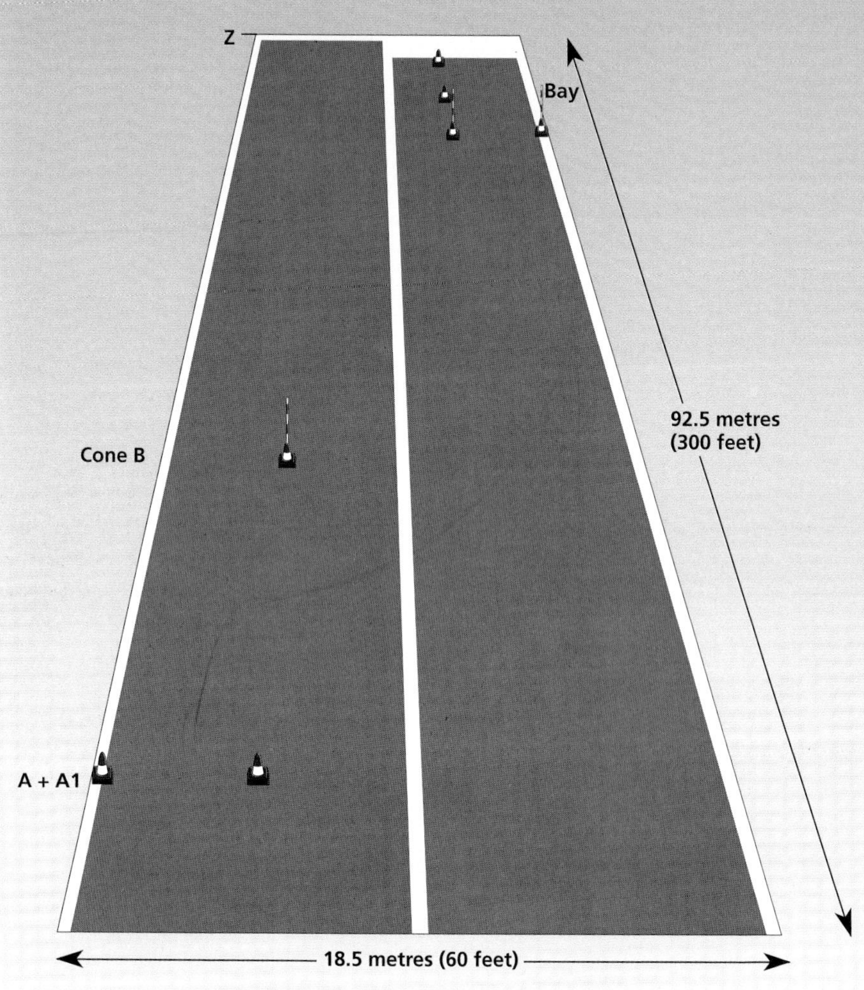
Z
Bay
92.5 metres
(300 feet)
Cone B
A + A1
18.5 metres (60 feet)

You'll be asked to carry out an off-road reversing exercise at the start of the test whether your test vehicle's coupled to a trailer or not. The examiner will use a diagram of the manoeuvring area to explain the exercise to you. If you take the test with a delegated company examiner the reversing exercise may consist of reversing into side roads on the left or right during the on-road part of the test.

The diagram opposite shows the area layout for this exercise. Starting from a fixed point (cones A and A1), you must keep your vehicle inside a clearly defined yellow boundary line so that

- The offside of your vehicle clears cone B
- You stop with the extreme rear of your vehicle within the solid (yellow painted) box area at the end of the bay, formed by cones

At some centres there's also a steel barrier along part of the boundary.

For vehicles without a significant front overhang, cone A is positioned on the area boundary line. For vehicles with a front overhang, the examiner has the discretion to move the cones. If the front axle is well back from the front of the bus or if it has a limited turning circle, cones A, A1 and B may be moved 1 metre (about 3 feet) further into the area from the boundary line.

## The distances

The manoeuvring area is 92.5 metres long by 18.5 metres wide (about 300 × 60 feet). The overall length for the manoeuvre will be five times the length of the vehicle.

A to A1 = 1.5 times the width of the vehicle

A to B = twice the length of the vehicle

B to line Z = 3 times the length of the vehicle

The width of the bay will be 1.5 times the width of the vehicle. The length of the bay will be based on the length of the vehicle. This can be varied at the discretion of the examiner so that the bay is one of the following lengths

- 1 metre (about 3 feet) longer than your vehicle
- The same length as your vehicle
- 1 metre shorter than your vehicle
- 2 metres (about 6 feet) shorter than your vehicle

You won't be told the precise length of the bay, as part of this exercise is designed to assess your judgement of the size of your vehicle.

## What the test requires

The exercise is designed to test your ability to manoeuvre your vehicle in a confined space. You must avoid the marker posts and reverse into a clearly defined bay

- Under control
- With reasonable accuracy
- With effective observation throughout

## Skills you should show

The examiner will ask you to drive your bus from where you parked it up to cones A and A1. When he or she signals you to do so, drive up to the cones and stop so that

- The front of your bus is between but not beyond the cones
- The bus is more or less parallel with the yellow boundary line

If you don't position the vehicle correctly the examiner may ask you to re-position your vehicle.

When you're asked you should then

- Steer so that the offside of your bus passes clear of cone B (which has a marker pole)
- Reverse across the area at a reasonable pace until the rear of your bus enters the bay formed by cones. (The two cones at the entrance to the bay will have marker poles.)
- Carefully control your use of the accelerator, clutch and footbrake throughout
- Steer to position your vehicle accurately
- Take effective observation throughout the exercise
- Make smooth continuous progress across the area
- Stop in the position explained to you by the examiner

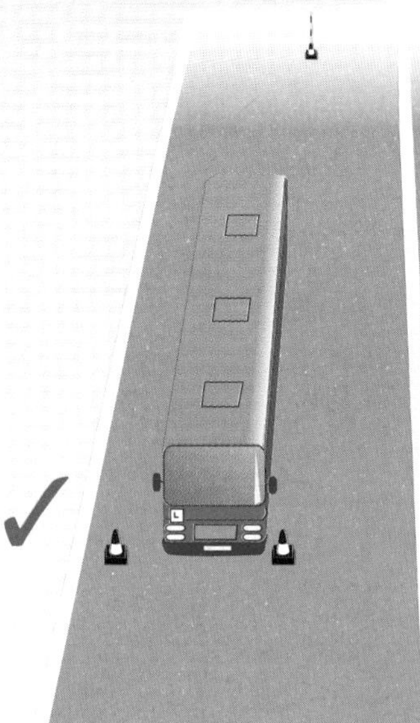

## Faults you should avoid

- Approaching the starting point too fast
- Not driving in a reasonably straight line as you approach
- Stopping beyond the first marker cones A and A1
- Turning the steering wheel the wrong way; turning too much or not enough when starting to reverse
- Over-steering so that the front offside wheel travels outside the yellow boundary line of the area
- Not taking effective observation or misjudging the position of your vehicle so that it hits (or is about to drive over) cone B and its marker pole
- Not taking effective observation or misjudging the position of your vehicle so that it hits (or is about to drive over) the cones or marker poles marking out the bay
- Allowing the wheel(s) of your vehicle to ride over the boundary lines of the bay or the area
- Making an incorrect judgement so that the rear of your vehicle is either short of or beyond the yellow box area at the end of the bay
- Taking excessive steering movements or 'shunts' to complete the manoeuvre. Since an overall high standard is expected, only a minimal number of shunts will be accepted
- Driving down the area ahead of a position level with cones A and A1 when you're 'shunting'. (This is because you'll have gone outside the limits set for your vehicle, i.e., five times its length, after starting the exercise.)
- Carrying out the manoeuvre at an excessively slow pace
- Leaving the cab in order to satisfy yourself of the vehicle's position

You should remember that, throughout the test, the examiner will be looking for expert handling of the controls.

This exercise usually takes place on the special manoeuvring area at the test centre and not on the public roads. If your test is conducted by a delegated examiner the braking exercise may be carried out on a quiet public road. The examiner will make sure that no other traffic is close enough to be inconvenienced.

You should make sure that, before you come to the test, there's no loose equipment in the interior of the bus or in luggage lockers. This could fly about and cause injury or damage during the exercise.

The examiner will be with you in the vehicle for this braking exercise. He or she will explain to you the signal to stop. Make sure that you clearly understand what it will be. The signal used will depend on the type of vehicle – it may be the examiner saying 'Stop!' loudly or it may be a bell signal.

## What the test requires

Two marker cones approximately 61 metres (200 feet) ahead will be pointed out to you. You should build up the speed of the vehicle to about 32 kph (20 mph). Only when the front of your vehicle passes between the two markers should you apply the brakes.

You should stop

- Quickly
- Safely
- Under full control

## Skills you should show

Stopping the vehicle

- As quickly as possible
- Under full control
- As safely as possible
- In a straight line

## Faults you should avoid

- Driving too slowly – less than 32 kph (20 mph)
- Braking too soon (anticipating the marker points or the stop signal)
- Braking too harshly, causing skidding
- Depressing the clutch too late, possibly stalling the engine
- Depressing the clutch too early, failing to take full advantage of any engine braking

If your bus is fitted with any additional braking controls, such as a retarder, exhaust brake or emergency air brake, you aren't expected to use them in this exercise. This is a test of your ability to stop quickly under normal circumstances.

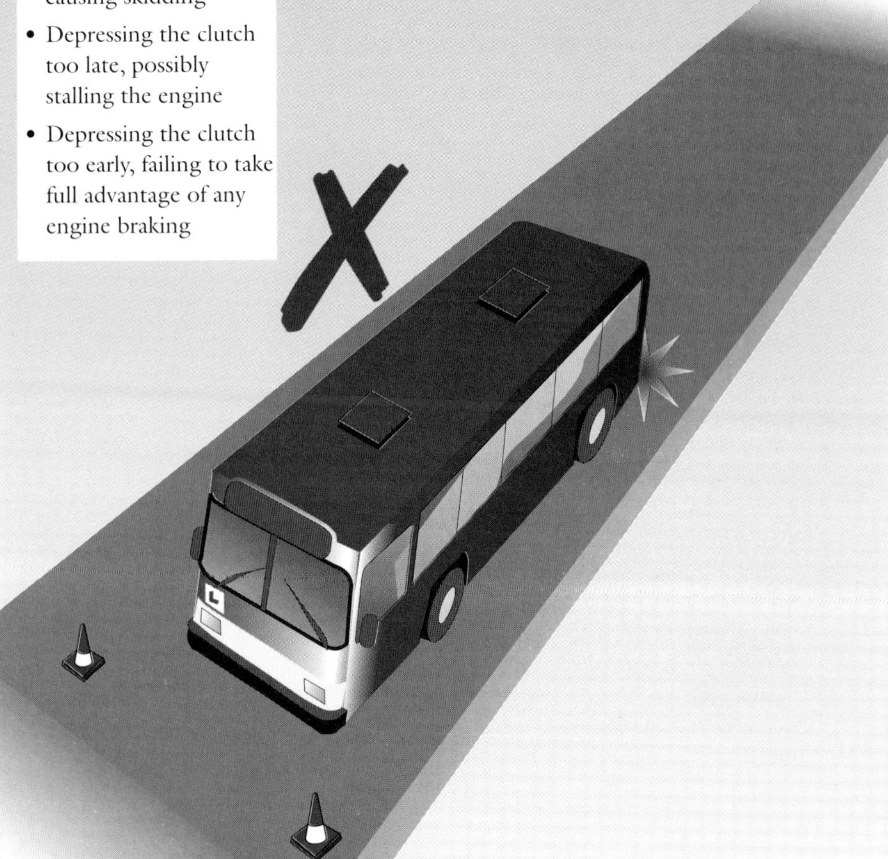

## What the test requires

You must show the examiner that you understand what all the controls do and that you can use them

- Smoothly
- Correctly
- Skilfully
- Safely
- At the right time

In particular, the examiner must be sure that you can properly control the

- Accelerator
- Clutch
- Footbrake
- Handbrake
- Steering
- Gears

Of course, if your vehicle has automatic transmission some of these won't apply to you. You must

- Understand what the controls do
- Be able to use them competently

## How your examiner will test you

For this aspect of driving there isn't a special exercise. The examiner will watch you carefully to see how you use these controls. There is, however, a special gear-changing exercise.

## Skills you should show

### Accelerator and clutch

- Balancing the accelerator and clutch to pull away smoothly
- Accelerating evenly to gain speed
- Releasing the accelerator smoothly to avoid erratic driving
- Depressing the clutch pedal just before the vehicle stops
- Engaging the clutch smoothly when moving away and changing gear

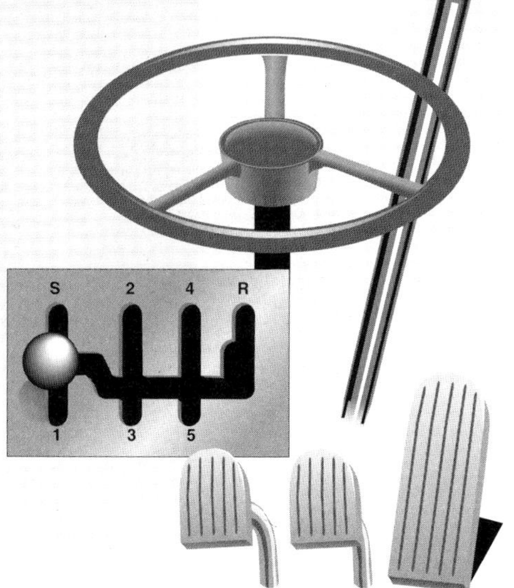

## Faults you should avoid

### Accelerator and clutch

- Loud over-revving, causing excessive engine noise and exhaust fumes. This could alarm or distract other road users
- Heavy, inappropriate acceleration followed by immediate braking
- Making the vehicle jerk and lurch through uncontrolled use of the accelerator or the clutch
- 'Riding' the clutch, that is, failing to take your foot off the pedal when you aren't using it
- Jerky and uncontrolled use of the clutch when moving off or changing gear

## Manual gearboxes

The gears are designed to assist the engine to deliver power under a variety of conditions. The lowest gears may only be necessary if a vehicle is loaded or when it's climbing steep gradients.

You should be aware of the manufacturer's advice for the particular vehicle that you drive. Some suggest that first gear should always be used when pulling away, others advise second. Following a manufacturer's advice can save your company a lot of money in minimising clutch and gearbox wear.

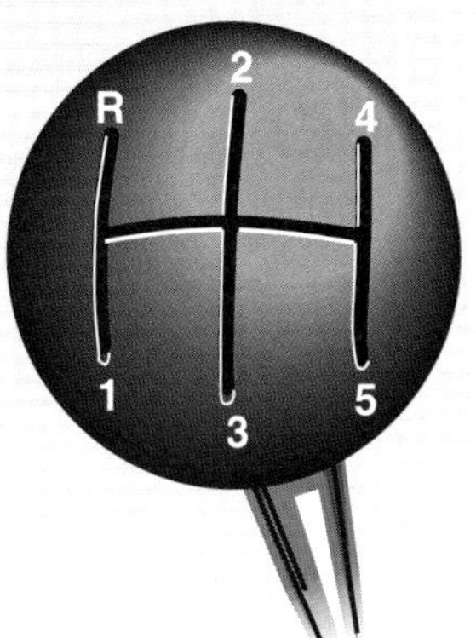


## Skills you should show

- Moving off in the most suitable gear
- Choosing the most appropriate gear for your speed and the road conditions
- Changing gear in good time before a hazard or junction
- Selecting the correct gear in good time when climbing or before descending a long hill. On gradients it's essential to plan well ahead

If you leave gear-changing until you're either losing or gaining too much speed you may have difficulty selecting the gear and maintaining control.

## Faults you should avoid

- Taking your eyes off the road when you change gear
- Holding onto the gear lever unnecessarily
- Selecting the 'wrong' gear
- 'Coasting' with the clutch pedal depressed or the gear lever in neutral

Coasting is particularly dangerous in vehicles fitted with air brakes. The engine-driven compressor won't replace air being exhausted as the brakes are applied, due to the engine only running at 'tick over' speed.

## Automatic gearboxes

Modern vehicles may be fitted with sophisticated gearing systems controlled by on-board computers. These systems sense the load, speed, gradient, etc. and select the most appropriate gear for the conditions. On such systems, the driver may only have to ease the accelerator or depress the clutch pedal to allow the system to engage the gear required.

Other automatic gearboxes are controlled by a very simple three-button system

- Forward (drive)
- Neutral
- Reverse

In spite of this simplicity, it's essential that you learn the correct way to use the system.

Some systems have a 'kick down' facility whereby a lower gear can be engaged to allow rapid acceleration (e.g., for overtaking). This is achieved by pressing the accelerator to the floor.

## Skills you should show

- Holding the vehicle firmly on the footbrake before pressing 'forward' to engage the drive. Some systems have interlocks that prevent 'drive' being engaged unless the brake pedal is depressed or the doors are closed, etc.
- Pressing the selector buttons only when the bus is completely stationary
- Making careful use of the accelerator to ensure smooth automatic gear-changing

## Faults you should avoid

- Engaging 'drive' whilst the engine revs are above 'tick over'
- Letting the bus remain stationary for long periods with 'forward' or 'reverse' engaged
- Forgetting to engage 'drive' before attempting to move off
- Not making proper use of any 'kick down' facility

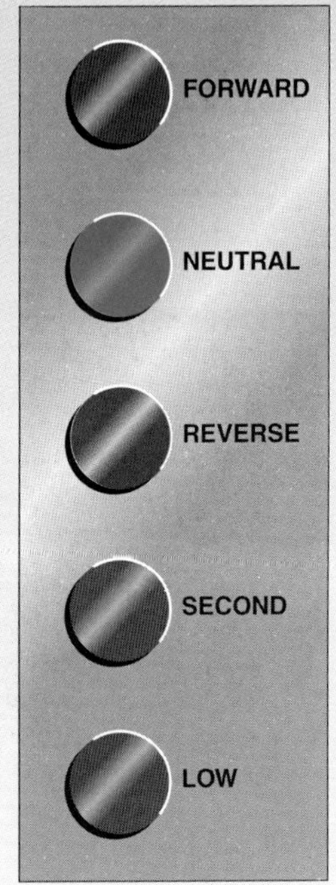

## Semi-automatic gearboxes

The system most commonly found on buses and coaches is one whereby the driver has full control over the gear selected but has no clutch pedal. This is often a 'pneumo-cyclic' gearbox, which consists of a number of electronic relays controlling air systems that make the actual gear changes. The gears are chosen by means of a 'gate' selector. When coupled with a fluid fly-wheel this system eliminates the need for the use of a clutch when pulling away, stopping or changing gear. However, smooth changes require some skill and practice to achieve.

Again, the most appropriate method of changing gear will depend on the manufacturer's advice for the particular vehicle. Most advise that, when changing between one gear and another, a brief pause be made when the lever is in neutral. The accelerator should be depressed to a level appropriate for the gear about to be engaged.

Usually semi-automatic gearboxes are coupled to diesel engines. Thus the amount of time needed in neutral to allow the engine revs to match the road speed needs careful consideration.

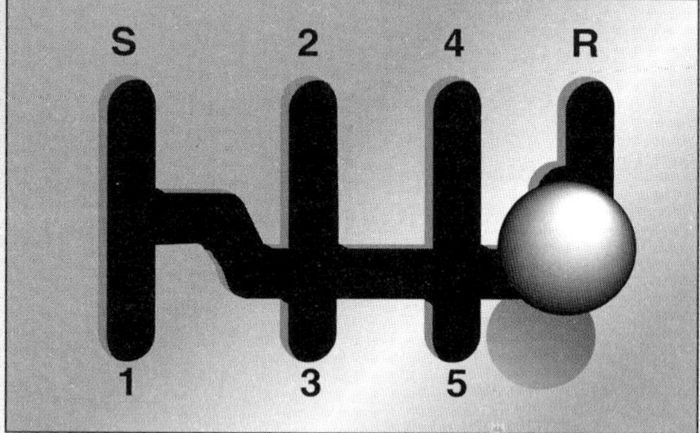


### Skills you should show

- Holding the vehicle firmly on the footbrake before engaging forward or reverse gears from a standstill. Some systems have interlocks that prevent 'drive' being engaged unless the brake pedal is depressed or the doors are closed, etc.
- Making careful use of the accelerator to ensure smooth gear-changing

### Faults you should avoid

- Engaging a forward or reverse gear from a standstill whilst the engine revs are above 'tick over'
- Letting the bus remain stationary for long periods with a forward or reverse gear engaged
- Forgetting to engage a gear before attempting to move off
- Not making proper use of the gear selector and accelerator

## The footbrake

Most buses, coaches and midibuses are equipped with air brake systems. This means there's frequently no direct relationship between the pressure applied to the pedal and the braking force exerted on the wheels. As a result good control is needed at all times when braking.

Vehicles equipped with disc brakes permit a technique in which the pressure applied to the brake pedal is proportional to the braking effect applied to the wheels. This is similar to the hydraulic system fitted to some minibuses.

Older vehicles may have vacuum brake systems, which have similar characteristics to air brakes.

Some other vehicles may have a system known as 'air over hydraulic', in which air pressure operates a hydraulic braking system. These are usually lighter vehicles and the system is designed to make the brakes less harsh.

## Skills you should show

- Braking in good time
- Braking lightly in most situations
- Braking progressively
- Using the correct technique for releasing pressure on the brake just before coming to rest. This allows you to stop the bus without jerks

## Faults you should avoid

- Braking harshly
- Excessive and prolonged use of the footbrake
- Braking and steering at the same time, unless you're already travelling at low speed
- Braking in a way that would cause passengers discomfort

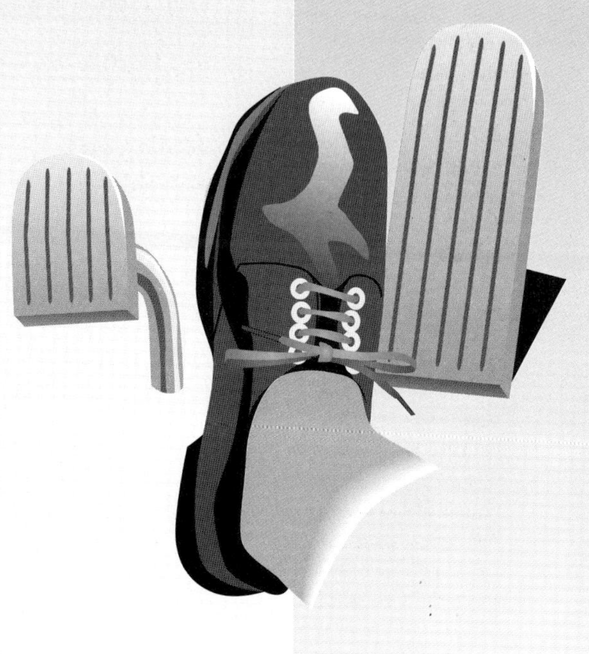

## The handbrake

Buses, coaches and minibuses are equipped with one of two types of handbrake.

### Mechanical

- Generally found on older or smaller vehicles
- Comprising a long lever with a button or, more usually, a squeeze-grip release, as in a car. The lever pulls a series of cables that apply the rear (or, more rarely, the front) brakes

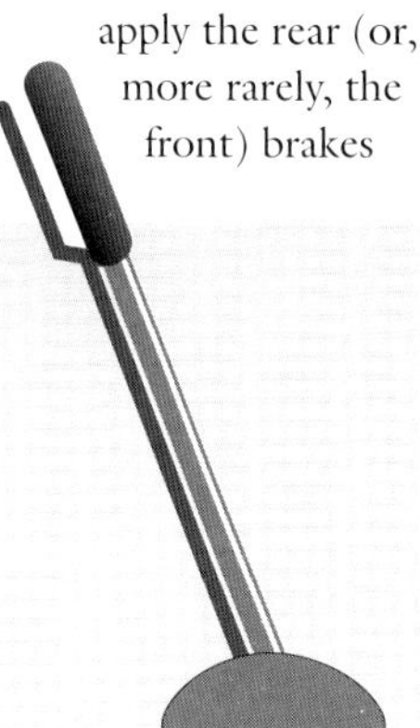

### Air-operated

- Fitted to vehicles with air or 'air over hydraulic' footbrake systems
- Operated by a small lever with a collar or a push-button release

## Skills you should show

- Knowing how and when to apply the handbrake
- Applying the handbrake before leaving the cab when you intend to secure the vehicle
- Co-ordinating your use of the handbrake and other controls in order to achieve smooth uphill starts

Some modern braking systems will apply a parking brake when the vehicle is brought to a stop by the footbrake. The handbrake is released in the normal way. You should know how to operate this system if it's fitted to a vehicle that you intend to drive.

## Faults you should avoid

- Applying the handbrake before the vehicle has stopped
- Attempting to move off with the handbrake still applied
- Using the 'park' position on the gear selector on automatic vehicles as a substitute for applying the handbrake. Only the gearbox locks when 'P' is engaged – the vehicle may be free to move when the next driver selects neutral to start the engine
- 'Holding' the vehicle on the clutch on uphill slopes (in manual buses and coaches). This can cause excessive clutch wear

The clutch isn't designed to prevent a vehicle weighing up to 18 tonnes from moving backwards. You should always apply the handbrake and carry out the correct uphill start procedure to avoid unnecessary wear and tear on the clutch.

## Emergency brakes

All vehicles are required to have at least two braking systems so that failure of one won't prevent the vehicle being brought to rest safely.

'Split' systems are often fitted to ensure that failure of one part of the normal braking system leaves other parts operational. 'Fail safe' systems can result in the automatic gradual application of all or some of the brakes if the driver ignores brake warning indicators.

Construction and Use regulations do require the driver to be able to apply all or part of the braking system in the event of footbrake failure. In simple terms this means that, if you press the footbrake and nothing happens, you must have another means of stopping. How you do this depends on the system fitted

- Mechanical handbrake: the handbrake can be applied progressively to bring the vehicle to a stop
- Emergency brake: a separate lever is provided on some older air- and vacuum-braked buses to allow progressive application of the brakes
- Air-operated handbrake: the brake is partially applied to allow progressive application of the brakes

During your training you should find out which method should be used with the vehicle that you drive. You should practise it in a safe place, preferably off the road and under expert supervision.

You must not use this method of braking at any time during your test. The braking exercise in the driving test requires a rapid, controlled stop, using the footbrake. It isn't an emergency stop exercise.

## Skills you should show

Normally it won't be necessary to demonstrate any emergency braking systems.

## Faults you should avoid

- Immediate full application of the brake
- Locking the wheels and skidding
- Coming to rest heavily in a way that may injure passengers

## Steering

The bus, coach or minibus you drive will probably have power-assisted steering. With power assistance the steering effort required is greatly reduced through the action of an engine-driven pump.

It's generally necessary to take corners more slowly when you don't have the benefit of power assistance, simply because the gearing at the steering wheel is lower and it takes more effort and time to turn it. The danger with power assistance is that the lack of effort required (and, in some cases, the lack of 'feel' transmitted back to the driver) can result in taking corners too quickly. This can put either safety or comfort at risk. You need to be aware of this.

## Skills you should show

- Placing your hands on the steering wheel in a position that's comfortable and which gives you full control at all times
- Keeping your steering movements steady and smooth
- Steering an accurate path and being aware of the 'swept path' that your vehicle will take

It's particularly important to take the correct path when driving a bus with long overhangs or limited ground clearance.

## Faults you should avoid

- Turning the wheel too early when turning a corner. You risk
  - cutting the corner when turning right, causing the rear wheel(s) to cut across the path of traffic waiting to emerge
  - striking the kerb when turning left
- Turning too late. You could put other road users at risk by
  - swinging wide at left turns
  - overshooting right turns
- Crossing your hands on the steering wheel, whenever possible
- Allowing the wheel to spin back after turning
- Resting your arm on the door

Remember, the stability of a bus can be affected by cornering too quickly.

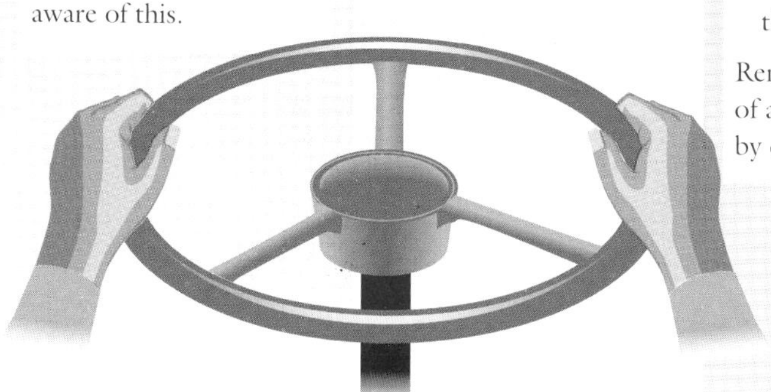

## You should understand

- The functions of all controls and switches that have a bearing on road safety, for example
  - indicators
  - lights
  - windscreen wipers
  - demisters
- The meaning of gauges or other displays on the instrument panel, especially
  - air pressure gauge(s)
  - speedometer
  - various warning lights/buzzers
  - on-board computer displays
  - braking systems failure warnings
  - bulb failure warnings
  - gear-selection indicators
- Time, speed and distance recording equipment, including
  - operating tachographs
  - completing tachograph charts
  - keeping records
  - the operation of any speed-limiting equipment fitted

## Safety checks

You should also be able to

- Carry out routine safety checks on
  - oil and coolant levels
  - tyre pressures
- Identify defects, especially with
  - steering
  - brakes
  - tyres
  - seat belts
  - lights
  - reflectors
  - horn
  - rear view mirrors
  - speedometer
  - exhaust system
  - direction indicators
  - windscreen, wipers and washers
  - wheel-nut security
- Understand the effects that any fault or defect will have on the handling of your vehicle

### Warning

Some bus manufacturers, but not all, fit wheel nuts that tighten clockwise on the nearside of the vehicle and anti-clockwise on the offside. Make sure that you know which thread is fitted to your vehicle before you attempt to tighten them. The consequences of getting it wrong are dangerous. In any case, it's much better to entrust this to trained mechanics, wherever possible, as the nuts should always be tightened to the specified torque. Some wheels are 'spigot'-mounted and require specialised knowledge when being removed or refitted.

## What the test requires

From a standstill, you must be able to move off safely and under control

- On the level
- From behind a parked vehicle
- On a hill
- Uphill and downhill

## How your examiner will test you

The examiner will watch your use of the controls each time you move off.

### Level and uphill starts

- Aim to co-ordinate your use of the controls so that the vehicle remains stationary momentarily when the handbrake is released, ready to move off
- Check all round for pedestrians and other road users. Move off if it's clear
- If there's more than a moment's delay between releasing the brake and moving off, reapply the handbrake and repeat the sequence when it's safe to do so

### Downhill starts

- Prevent the vehicle from moving when you release the handbrake by applying the footbrake first

### Angle starts

- Ensure that you apply sufficient steering to pass the parked vehicle safely
- Ensure that you won't endanger traffic when you move away

## Skills you should show

- Watching the road ahead and behind in order to predict an opportunity to move
- Selecting an appropriate gear or 'drive' and preparing the vehicle to move when you can see that you'll shortly be able to move off
- Checking whether it's safe to move off and informing other road users of your intentions by
  - using your mirrors
  - signalling, if necessary
  - releasing the handbrake
- Looking round just before moving off for
  - other vehicles
  - cyclists
  - pedestrians or animals outside the range of your mirrors
- Checking the road immediately ahead and moving off under control, making balanced and safe use of the
  - accelerator
  - clutch
  - brakes
  - steering

## Faults you should avoid

- Forgetting to engage a forward gear
- Moving off whilst looking behind
- Failing to co-ordinate your use of the controls to achieve a safe, comfortable start
- Endangering other road users when moving off
- Not co-ordinating the accelerator, clutch and handbrake, with the result that the vehicle
  - stalls
  - rolls backwards on an uphill slope
  - surges away

As you move off and the position of the vehicle on the road changes, recheck all your mirrors to ensure that all is well, both outside and inside the vehicle. However, don't allow this to distract you when your attention should be on the road ahead.

## How your examiner will test you

The examiner will ask you to pull up at a convenient place to carry out the gear-changing exercise (usually at an early stage in the test).

You'll be asked to move off in the lowest gear and change up to each gear in turn until you reach a gear the examiner considers appropriate for your vehicle. This will depend on the gearbox fitted. The examiner will make sure that you understand which gear should be reached.

When you've reached the agreed gear the examiner will want to see you change back down into each gear in turn, driving for a short distance in each gear until you reach the lowest gear again.

You won't be asked to use anything other than the normal gears appropriate to your vehicle.

The gear-changing exercise enables the examiner to see whether you engage the lower gears competently. An opportunity for you to demonstrate this skill may not occur naturally during the test.

## Skills you should show

- Moving off smoothly in the lowest gear
- Changing up to the next gear as soon as the correct speed is reached
- Smooth, unhurried and precise gear changes
- Matching the road speed of the vehicle to the lower gear, when changing down, by careful use of the footbrake, if necessary

Throughout this exercise you must

- Use effective observation, especially before moving off and slowing down
- Give any signal that may be appropriate
- Use the controls skilfully to ensure smooth engagement of the gears

## Faults you should avoid

- Not showing sufficient consideration for other road users before moving off, during the exercise or when slowing down by
  - forgetting to check the mirrors
  - not acting sensibly in response to the actions of other drivers
  - not signalling to inform other road users before moving off or slowing down
- Jerky use of the accelerator or clutch
- Not starting off in the lowest gear
- Not selecting the next gear in sequence
- Not being able to engage a gear
- Not slowing the vehicle down enough before selecting a lower gear

Mirrors are one of the best aids to road safety. They help you to avoid causing problems to other road users and allow you to predict when to take action safely.

Try not to think of mirror checks as something you do because you've been told to. The important point isn't that you've looked in the mirrors, but that you've gained additional information to help you to drive safely.

Try to time your mirror checks to allow time to assess what you see before taking any action.

## Sequence of mirror checks

Professional drivers develop a technique for checking mirrors whilst remaining fully aware of what's happening ahead. Whatever method you adopt the examiner will observe how you use the mirrors and whether you act sensibly on what you see.

When you're on the road hazards often occur together, or one immediately after another. They may also happen just when the need to begin a manoeuvre to deal with them occurs.

You must ensure that you observe every potential danger and are fully prepared to deal with it, if it occurs.

The sequence of checks has to be adapted as situations develop. In reality, it takes only moments to carry out and should become second nature without the need to constantly analyse what you're doing.

### Order of checks

- Identify the hazard that gives rise to the need to manoeuvre
- Assess where the greatest potential danger lies in the intended manoeuvre – to the right or to the left of your vehicle. Check that mirror first
- Check the mirror on the other side
- As your eyes return to the road ahead reassess the hazard and, if you have an interior mirror that allows you to see what's happening behind, check the position of following traffic
- Check the first mirror again and, as your eyes return to the road ahead, assess what you've seen and signal if necessary
- Carry out the manoeuvre, if it's still safe to do so, rechecking the mirrors as necessary

**Moving out to pass a parked car**

You see a parked car some distance ahead.

The primary danger is that someone may attempt to overtake you as you need to move out. Check the offside mirror.

Check the nearside mirror.

Check that the parked car hasn't moved away, or that you'll need to give it extra room because someone's about to get out.

Will you need to wait for approaching traffic?

Look to see what traffic is following you by checking the offside mirror.

Has the situation ahead changed? Signal right, if necessary.

Begin to move out if it's safe to do so, or wait if it isn't

Keep checking how the situation develops.

## What the test requires

Make sure that you use your mirrors effectively

- Before any manoeuvre
- To keep up to date on what's happening behind you

Check carefully before

- Moving off
- Signalling
- Changing direction
- Turning left or right
- Overtaking or changing lanes
- Increasing speed
- Slowing down or stopping
- Opening any offside door

Check again in the nearside mirror after

- Passing parked vehicles
- Passing horse riders, motorcyclists or cyclists
- Passing any pedestrians standing close to the kerb
- Passing any vehicle you've just overtaken and before moving back to the left

## How your examiner will test you

For this aspect of driving there isn't a special exercise. The examiner will watch your use of mirrors as you drive.

## Skills you should show

- Establishing good habits by
  - looking before you signal
  - looking and signalling before you act
  - acting sensibly and safely on what you see in the mirrors
- Being aware that the mirrors won't show everything behind you
- Checking your nearside mirror, every time, after passing
  - parked vehicles
  - vulnerable road users
  - vehicles you've just overtaken
- Always being as aware of what's happening behind and alongside as you are of what's going on ahead
- Always being aware of the effect your vehicle has on any vulnerable road users that you may pass

## Faults you should avoid

- Manoeuvring without checking the mirrors first
- Not acting on what you see when you look in the mirrors
- Taking action at the same time as looking in the mirrors, instead of as a result of what you see in them
- Looking in the mirrors at an inappropriate moment so that you fail to observe changes in the situation ahead

Remember, just looking isn't enough. Acting sensibly on what you see is more important. Always use the MSM/PSL routine

- Mirrors
- Signal
- Manoeuvre
  - Position
  - Speed
  - Look

## What the test requires

You must give clear signals in good time so that other road users know what you intend to do next. This is particularly important with long PCVs because other road users may not understand the position you need to move into

- Before turning left
- Before turning right
- At roundabouts
- To move off at an angle
- Before reversing into an opening

You must only use the signals shown in *The Highway Code* as any others may be misunderstood.

Any signal you give must help other road users to

- Understand what you intend to do next
- Take appropriate action

Always check that you've cancelled an indicator signal as soon as it's safe to do so.

## How your examiner will test you

For this aspect of driving there isn't a special exercise. The examiner will watch carefully to see how you use signals in your driving.

## Skills you should show

Give any signals

- Clearly
- At the appropriate time
- By indicator
- By arm, if necessary

Make sure that any signal you give is visible long enough so that other road users see and understand its meaning.

## Faults you should avoid

- Giving misleading or incorrect signals
- Omitting to cancel signals
- Waving on pedestrians to cross in front of your vehicle (neither you nor they may have seen a dangerous situation, which you're 'inviting' them towards)
- Giving signals other than those shown in *The Highway Code*

## What the test requires

You must have a thorough knowledge of traffic signs, signals and road markings. You should be able to

- Recognise them in good time
- Take appropriate action on them

At the start of the road section of the PCV driving test the examiner will ask you to continue to follow the road ahead, unless traffic signs indicate otherwise or unless you're asked to turn left or right. You'll be given any direction to turn in good time. If you aren't sure, ask the examiner to repeat the direction.

## Skills you should show

### Traffic lights

You must

- Comply with traffic lights
- Approach at such a speed that you can stop, if necessary, under full control
- Only move forward at a green traffic light if
  - it's clear for you to do so
  - by doing so your vehicle won't block the junction

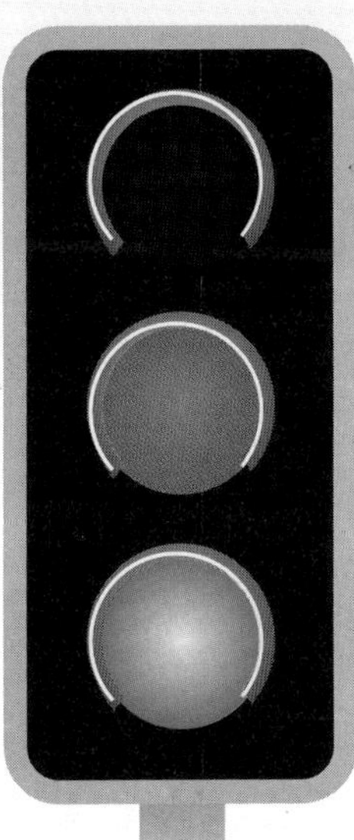

### Authorised persons

You must comply with signals given by

- Police officers
- Traffic wardens
- School crossing patrols
- Any authorised person controlling traffic, e.g., at road repairs

### Other road users

You must watch for signals given by other road users and

- React safely
- Take appropriate action
- Anticipate their actions
- Give signals to any traffic following your vehicle that may not be able to see the signals given by a road user ahead of you. This is particularly important when a vehicle or rider ahead is intending to turn right, and the size of your vehicle prevents traffic behind you from seeing their signal.

The examiner will be looking for a high standard of driving from an experienced driver displaying safe, confident driving techniques. You aren't a learner driver and you won't pass the test if you drive hesitantly or in a way that shows you aren't fully in control of your vehicle.

Because you're an experienced driver and are expected to drive accordingly, you must

- Select a safe speed to suit road, weather and traffic conditions
- Move away at junctions as soon as it's safe to do so
- Avoid stopping unnecessarily
- Make progress when conditions permit

## How your examiner will test you

For this aspect of driving there isn't a special exercise. The examiner will watch your driving and will expect to see you

- Making reasonable progress where conditions allow
- Keeping up with the traffic flow when it's safe and legal to do so
- Making positive, safe decisions as you make progress

## Skills you should show

- Driving at the appropriate speed, depending on the
  - type of road
  - traffic conditions
  - weather conditions and visibility
- Approaching all hazards at a safe speed without
  - being unduly cautious
  - holding up following traffic unnecessarily

## Faults you should avoid

- Driving so slowly that you hinder other traffic
- Being over-cautious or hesitant
- Stopping when you can see that it's obviously clear and safe to make progress

## What the test requires

You should make good progress when possible, taking into consideration

- The type of road
- The volume of traffic
- The weather conditions and the state of the road surface
- The braking characteristics of your vehicle
- Speed limits that apply to your vehicle
- Any hazards associated with the time of day (school times, etc.)

## How your examiner will test you

For this aspect of driving there isn't a special exercise. The examiner will watch carefully your control of speed as you drive.

## Skills you should show

- Taking great care in the use of speed
- Driving at the appropriate speed to the traffic conditions
- Being sure that you can stop safely in the distance that you can see to be clear
- Leaving a safe separation distance between your vehicle and the traffic ahead
- Allowing extra stopping distance on wet or slippery road surfaces
- Observing the speed limits that apply to your vehicle
- Driving sensibly and anticipating any hazards that could arise
- Allowing for other road users making mistakes

## Faults you should avoid

- Driving too fast for the conditions
  - road
  - traffic
  - weather
- Exceeding speed limits
- Varying your speed erratically
- Having to brake hard to avoid a situation ahead
- Approaching bends, traffic signals and any other hazards at too high a speed

Always keep a safe separation distance between you and the vehicle in front.

## What the test requires

You must always drive at such a speed that you can stop safely in the distance that you can see to be clear.

In good weather conditions, leave a gap of at least 1 metre (about 3 feet) for each mph of your speed, or a two-second time gap.

In bad conditions, leave at least double that distance, or a four-second time gap.

In slow-moving congested traffic it may not be practical to leave as much space, but you must always be sure that you can stop safely – whatever happens.

## How your examiner will test you

For this aspect of driving there isn't a special exercise. The examiner will watch carefully and take account of your

- Use of the MSM/PSL routine
- Anticipation
- Reaction to changing road and traffic conditions
- Handling of the controls

## Skills you should show

- Being able to judge a safe separation distance between you and the vehicle ahead
- Showing correct use of the MSM routine, especially before reducing speed
- Avoiding the need to brake sharply if the vehicle in front slows down or stops
- Taking extra care when your view ahead is limited by large vehicles, such as other buses or lorries

Watch out for

- Brake lights ahead
- Direction indicators
- Vehicles ahead braking without warning

## Faults you should avoid

- Following too closely or 'tailgating'
- Braking suddenly
- Swerving to avoid the vehicle in front, which may be slowing down or stopping
- Not leaving side road junctions clear when a queue of traffic stops

The traffic situation can change from second to second, depending on the time of day, the location and the density of traffic. Sometimes you can see that a situation is obviously going to turn dangerous. The skilful driver anticipates what might happen.

As the driver of a bus, coach or minibus you must constantly drive with this sense of awareness and anticipation. Ask yourself

- What's happening ahead?
- What are other road users doing, or about to do?
- Do I need to
  - speed up?
  - slow down?
  - prepare to stop?
  - change direction?

It's essential to be fully alert at all times and to scan the road ahead constantly. By doing this you'll remain in control of both the situation and your vehicle.

In fast-moving traffic you'll need to be constantly checking and rechecking the scene around you. It's essential to recognise well in advance the mistakes other road users may be about to make.

## What's a hazard?

When you're moving, a hazard is any situation that could involve adjusting speed or altering course. Look well ahead for

- Road junctions or roundabouts
- Parked vehicles
- Cyclists or horse riders
- Pedestrian crossings

By identifying the hazard early enough you'll have time to take the appropriate action.

When you're stationary, a hazard can be created by the actions of other road users around you. Watch for

- Pedestrians crossing in front
- Cyclists or motor-cyclists moving up alongside
- Drivers edging up on the nearside before you make a left turn
- Vehicles pulling up close behind when you intend to reverse

Stay on the alert and watch what's happening around you.

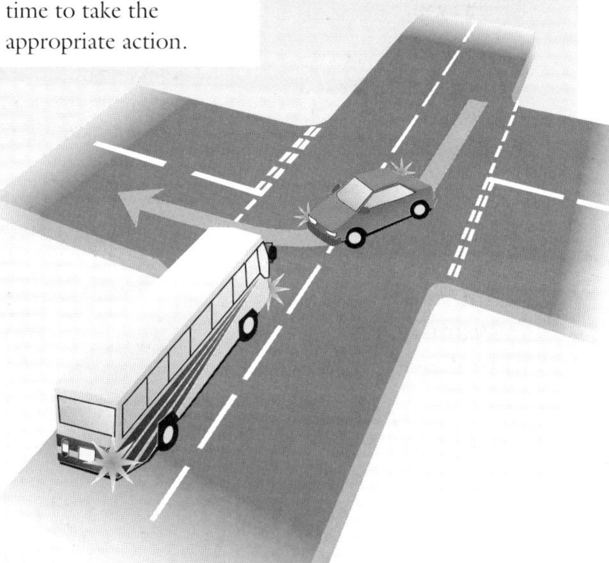

## Skills you should show

### Pedestrians

- Give way to pedestrians when turning from one road into another, or when entering premises such as bus or railway stations, schools, etc.
- Take extra care with the
  - very young
  - disabled
  - elderly

  They may not realise you won't be able to stop suddenly

You must be even more vigilant when driving through shopping areas, for example, where there are often large numbers of people waiting to cross at corners. Drive slowly and considerately when you need to enter any pedestrianised areas.

### Cyclists

Take extra care when

- Crossing cycle lanes
- You can see a cyclist near the rear of your vehicle or moving up along the nearside as you're about to turn left
- Approaching any children on cycles
- There are gusty wind conditions

### Motorcyclists

Watch for motorcyclists

- Filtering in slow traffic streams
- Moving up along the side of your vehicle
- Especially when you're about to move out at junctions

**Think once**

**Think twice**

**Think bike.**

## Horse riders and animals

Remember, the size, noise and sometimes even the colour of your vehicle can unsettle even the best mannered horse. Watch young, possibly inexperienced, riders closely for signs of any difficulty with their mounts. Give horse riders as much room as you can.

Avoid the need to rev the engine until you're clear of the animal. Several light applications of the brakes as you approach should ensure that the air brake system relief valve doesn't blow off just as you're level with the animal.

React in good time to anyone herding animals. Look out for warning signs or signals in rural districts.

## Faults you should avoid

- Sounding the horn unnecessarily
- Revving the engine, deliberately
- Causing the air brakes to 'hiss' by heavy applications
- Edging forward when pedestrians are crossing in front of your vehicle
- Any signs of irritation or aggression towards other road users, especially the more vulnerable

## What the test requires

You should

- Normally keep well to the left
- Keep clear of parked vehicles
- Avoid weaving in and out between parked vehicles
- Position your vehicle correctly for the direction you intend to take
- Obey road markings, especially
  - left- and right-turn arrows at junctions
  - when approaching roundabouts
  - in one-way streets
  - bus lanes
  - road markings for PCVs or LGVs approaching arched or narrow low bridges

With long PCVs, only straddle lane markings or move over to the left or right when necessary to avoid mounting the kerb or colliding with lamp-posts, traffic signs, etc.

## How your examiner will test you

For this aspect of driving there isn't a special exercise. The examiner will watch carefully to see that you

- Use the MSM routine
- Select the correct lane in good time

## Skills you should show

- Using the MSM/PSL routine correctly
- Planning ahead and choosing the correct lane in good time
- Positioning your vehicle sensibly, even if there aren't any lane markings

Always remember that other road users may not understand what you intend to do next. Watch them carefully and ensure that you signal in good time.

## Faults you should avoid

- Driving too close to the kerb
- Driving too close to the centre of the road
- Changing lanes at the last moment or without good reason
- Hindering other road users by being incorrectly positioned or in the wrong lane
- Straddling lanes or lane markings when it's unnecessary
- Using the size of your vehicle to block other road users from making progress
- Cutting across the path of other road users in another lane at roundabouts

The size of your vehicle and the difficulties that may arise when manoeuvring it means that it's essential to make the correct decisions at road junctions.

Never drive into a situation that you can't see a clear path through. If you drive your vehicle into a blocked road any traffic building up behind will prevent you from reversing out, leaving you in an impossible position. Similarly, if you need to wait for an obstruction to clear, stop in a position that allows you an escape route if at all possible.

## What the test requires

You should

- Use the MSM/PSL routine in good time on the approach to junctions
- Assess the situation correctly, so that you can position the vehicle to negotiate the junction safely
- Take as much room as you need on approach to see the road space available. There may not be enough room for a wide swing in the road that you're entering
- Take advantage of any improved vision from the driving position in your vehicle and stop or proceed as necessary
- Be aware of any lane markings and the fact that your vehicle may have to occupy part of the lane alongside
- Try to position in good time in one-way streets
- Make sure you take effective observation before emerging at any road junction
- Use your mirrors to observe the rear wheels of your vehicle as you drive into and out of the junction
- Correctly assess the speed of oncoming vehicles before crossing or entering roads with fast-moving traffic
- Always allow for the fact that you'll need time to build up speed in the new road

If you're crossing a dual carriageway or turning right onto one don't move forward unless you can clear the centre reservation safely. If your vehicle is too long for the gap, wait until it's clear from both sides and there's a safe opportunity to go.

## How your examiner will test you

For this aspect of driving there isn't a special exercise. The examiner will watch carefully and take account of your

- Use of the MSM/PSL routine
- Position and speed on approach
- Observation and judgement

As an aid to remembering the correct routine, think of the word LADEN

- **L**ook well ahead on approach
- **A**ssess conditions at the junction
- **D**ecide when it's safe to go
- **E**merge from (or enter) the junction safely
- **N**egotiate the hazard (junction) safely

This acronym recognises the techniques required of the PCV driver, and expands on the car driver's Look, Assess, Decide, Act (LADA) procedure, outlined in *The Driving Manual* (The Stationery Office).

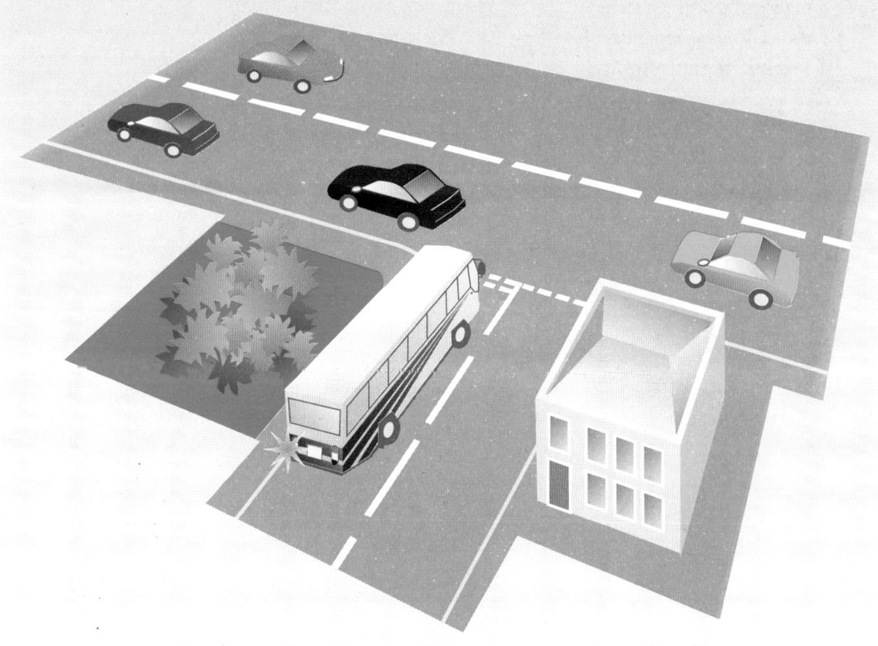

## What the test requires

Roundabouts can vary in size and complexity but the object of all of them is to allow traffic to keep moving, wherever possible.

Some roundabouts are so complex that they require traffic lights to control the volume of traffic, whilst at others signals operate at peak periods only.

At the majority of roundabouts the approaching traffic is required to give way to the traffic approaching from the right. However, at some locations the 'give way' signs and markings apply to traffic already on the roundabout. You must be aware of these differences.

## Skills you should show

You should plan your approach well in advance and use the MSM/PSL routine in good time. With buses, it's essential to adopt the appropriate lane, depending on the exit you intend to take and the size of your vehicle.

### Lane discipline

- Plan well ahead
- Look out for traffic signs as you approach
- Have a clear picture of the exit you need to take
- Look out for the number of exits before yours
- Either follow the lane markings, as far as possible, or select the lane most suitable to the size of your vehicle
- Signal your intentions clearly and in good time
- Avoid driving into the roundabout too close to the right-hand kerb
- As it isn't always possible to keep your vehicle within road markings, make frequent mirror checks to ensure that you aren't endangering others
- Accurately assess the speed and intentions of traffic approaching from the right

Always watch any vehicle in front when you're about to enter the roundabout. Make sure that it's moved off while you look to the right. Drivers sometimes change their minds at the last moment. Many rear-end collisions take place in just these circumstances.

Unless lane markings or road signs indicate otherwise you should follow the procedure noted here when turning left or right, or when going straight ahead.

**Turning left**

- Check your mirrors
- Give a left-turn signal in good time as you approach
- Approach in the left-hand lane. With a long vehicle you might need to take up some of the lane on your right, depending on how sharp or narrow the exit turn is
- Adopt a path that ensures your rear wheels don't mount the kerb
- Give way to traffic approaching from the right, if necessary
- Use the nearside mirror(s) to be sure that no cyclists or motorcyclists are trapped on the nearside
- Use the offside mirror to check that no passing vehicle will be hit when the rear overhang swings out as you begin to turn
- Continue to signal through the turn
- Look well ahead for traffic islands/bollards in the middle of your exit road, which will restrict the width available to you

**Going ahead**

(Up to 12 o'clock)

- Approach in the left-hand lane unless blocked or clearly marked for 'left turn' only
- Don't give a signal on approach (other than brake lights, if you need to reduce speed)
- Try to stay in the lane if possible, depending on the length of your vehicle
- Keep checking the mirrors. Be aware that other road users may not anticipate the 'swept path' of your vehicle. Be prepared to stop if they don't, as swerving will normally make matters worse
- Indicate left as you pass the exit just before the one that you intend to take
- Look well ahead for traffic islands/bollards in the centre of your exit road
- Make sure that the rear wheels don't mount the kerb as you leave the roundabout

### Turning right or full circle

- Look well ahead and use the MSM/PSL routine in good time
- Signal right in good time before moving over to the right on approach. Watch for any vehicles, especially motorcycles, accelerating up on the offside of your vehicle
- If there are two lanes available for turning right use the left-hand of the two lanes (when driving a long vehicle)
- When you need extra space, occupy part of the lane to your left if one lane only is marked for 'right turn'. Do this on the approach and through the roundabout
- Make frequent mirror checks
- Only enter the roundabout when you're sure that it's safe to emerge
- Keep checking for traffic coming from your right

Don't pull out across the path of any vehicle closely approaching from the right. Not only could the approaching vehicle be travelling at speed, but it could also be moving on a curved course so any sudden braking would be likely to send the vehicle into a skid.

- Use the mirrors to observe traffic coming round with you on the nearside, and also to check that your rear wheels are keeping clear of the kerb on the roundabout itself
- Change your signal to 'left turn' as you pass the exit before the one you wish to take

This procedure is useful when you need to turn a PCV round.

### Road surfaces

Roundabouts are junctions where considerable braking and acceleration takes place. The road surface can become slippery and polished, especially in wet weather.

Ensure that all braking and speed reduction is done in good time.

If you can see that it's clear to enter the roundabout, do so – provided you won't cause any traffic from your right to brake or swerve.

### Cyclists and horse riders

It's often safest for cyclists and horse riders to take the outside path when turning right at large roundabouts. Watch for any signals and give them as much room as you safely can.

### Mini-roundabouts

The same rules and procedures apply at mini-roundabouts as at full-scale roundabouts.

- Give way to traffic approaching from the right
- Because of the restricted space both entering and leaving these locations, it's essential to keep a constant check on the mirrors
- The rear of a long vehicle can easily 'clip' a car waiting to enter a mini-roundabout
- It's most unlikely that PCVs will be able to turn at a mini-roundabout without driving over the marked centre area
- Position your vehicle so that it doesn't mount the kerb at the entrance or exit

### Double mini-roundabouts

These require even more care and planning since traffic will often back up from one to the other at busy times. Make sure that there's room for you to move forward and that, by doing so, your vehicle won't block the whole system.

Although traffic is advised not to carry out U-turn manoeuvres at a mini-roundabout, be alert for any oncoming traffic doing so.

Avoid any signals that might confuse. Because of the limited space and the comparatively short amount of time that it takes to negotiate a mini-roundabout, it's important to give only signals that will help other road users.

If you have to drive over a raised mini-roundabout do so slowly and carefully so as not to damage your vehicle or cause discomfort to your passengers.

At any roundabout, cancel your indicator signal as soon as you've completed the manoeuvre.

### Multiple roundabouts

At a number of (usually well-known) locations complex roundabout systems have been designed, which incorporate a mini-roundabout at each exit.

The main thing to remember at such places is that traffic is travelling in all directions.

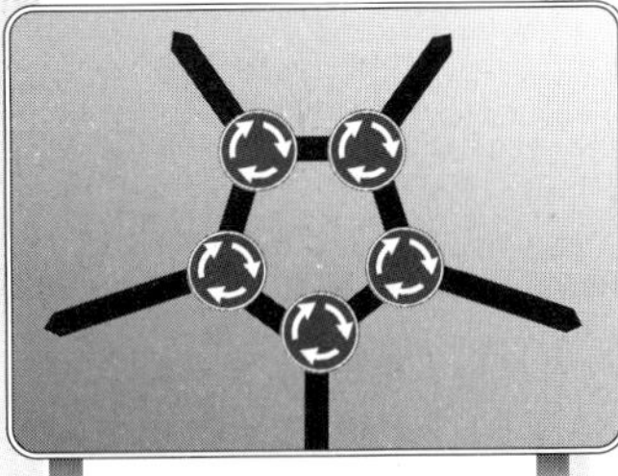

Sometimes mini-roundabouts are sited at what were formerly T-junctions. These junctions can be at a variety of angles so you should adopt the safest position on approach (even if technically 'going ahead'). Give an appropriate signal to other road users.

## What the test requires

When overtaking, you must

- Look well ahead for any hazards, such as
  - oncoming traffic
  - bends
  - junctions
  - road markings
  - traffic signs
  - the vehicle in front about to overtake
  - any gradient
- Assess the speed of the vehicle you intend to overtake
- Assess the speed differential of the two vehicles. This will indicate how long the manoeuvre could take
- Allow enough room to overtake safely
- Avoid the need to 'cut in' on the vehicle you've just overtaken

## How your examiner will test you

For this aspect of driving there isn't a special exercise. The examiner will watch carefully and take account of your

- Use of the MSM/PSL routine
- Reactions to road and traffic conditions
- Handling of the controls
- Choice of safe opportunities to overtake

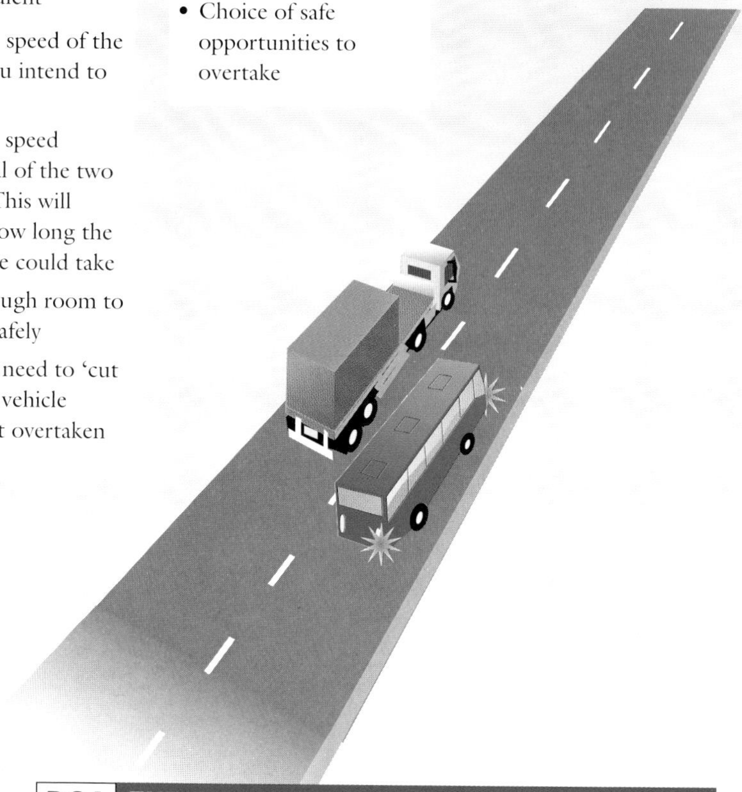

## Skills you should show

You must be able to assess all the factors that will help you to decide if you can overtake safely, such as

- Oncoming traffic
- The type of road (single or dual carriageway)
- The speed of the vehicle ahead
- If you can overtake before reaching any continuous white line on your side of the road
- How far ahead the road is clear
- Whether the road will remain clear
- Whether your mirror checks show that there's traffic behind about to overtake

Overtake only when you can do so

- Safely
- Legally
- Without causing other road users to slow down or alter course

## Faults you should avoid

You must not overtake when

- Your view of the road ahead isn't clear
- You would have to exceed the speed limit
- To do so would cause other road users to slow down, stop or swerve
- There are signs or road markings that prohibit overtaking

## What the test requires

You must be able to meet and deal with oncoming traffic safely and confidently, especially

- On narrow roads
- Where there are obstructions such as parked cars
- Where you have to move into the path of oncoming vehicles

## How your examiner will test you

For this aspect of driving there isn't a special exercise. The examiner will watch carefully and take account of your

- Use of the MSM/PSL routine
- Reactions to road and traffic conditions
- Handling of the controls

## Skills you should show

- Showing sound judgement when meeting oncoming traffic
- Being decisive when stopping and moving off
- Stopping in a position that allows you to move out smoothly when the way is clear
- Allowing adequate clearance when passing stationary vehicles. Slow down if you have to pass close to them

Be on the alert for

- Doors opening
- Children running out
- Pedestrians stepping out from between parked vehicles or round the front of other buses
- Vehicles pulling out without warning

## Faults you should avoid

- Causing other vehicles to
  - slow down
  - swerve
  - stop
- Passing dangerously close to parked vehicles
- Using the size of your vehicle to force other road users to give way

## What the test requires

You must be able to cross the path of oncoming traffic safely and with confidence. You'll need to be able to carry out this manoeuvre safely when you intend to

- Turn right at a road junction
- Enter bus stations or garages on the right-hand side of the road

You should

- Use the MSM/PSL routine on approach
- Position the vehicle correctly. The width and type of road and the length of the vehicle will affect this
- Accurately assess the speed of any approaching traffic
- Wait, if necessary
- Observe the road or entrance you're about to turn into
- Watch for any pedestrians

## How your examiner will test you

For this aspect of driving there isn't a special exercise. The examiner will watch carefully and take account of your judgement of oncoming traffic.

## Skills you should know

- Making safe and confident decisions about when to turn across the path of vehicles approaching from the opposite direction
- Ensuring that the road or entrance is clear for you to enter
- Being confident that your vehicle won't endanger any road user waiting to emerge from the right
- Accurately assessing whether it's safe to enter the road or entrance
- Showing courtesy and consideration to other road users, especially pedestrians

## Faults you should avoid

- Turning across the path of oncoming road users, causing them to
  - slow down
  - swerve
  - brake
- Cutting the corner so that you endanger vehicles waiting to emerge
- Overshooting the turn so that the front wheels mount the kerb

## What the test requires

You must be able to

- Recognise the different types of pedestrian crossing
- Show courtesy and consideration towards pedestrians
- Stop safely, when necessary

## How your examiner will test you

For this aspect of driving there isn't a special exercise. The examiner will watch carefully to see that you

- Recognise the pedestrian crossing in good time
- Use the MSM/PSL routine
- Stop when necessary
- Are especially alert when crossings are sited
  - near schools
  - in shopping areas
  - at or near junctions

## Skills you should show

- Approaching all crossings at a controlled speed
- Stopping safely, when necessary
- Moving off when you're sure it's safe to do so

### Controlled crossings

These crossings may be controlled by

- Traffic signals at junctions
- Police officers
- Traffic wardens
- School crossing patrols

### Zebra crossings

These crossings are recognised by

- Black and white stripes across the road
- A row of studs along each edge of the black and white stripes
- Flashing amber beacons at both sides of the road
- Zigzag markings on the road on both sides of the crossing

You must

- Slow down and stop if there's anyone on the crossing
- Slow down and be prepared to stop if anyone is waiting to cross or will reach the crossing before you do

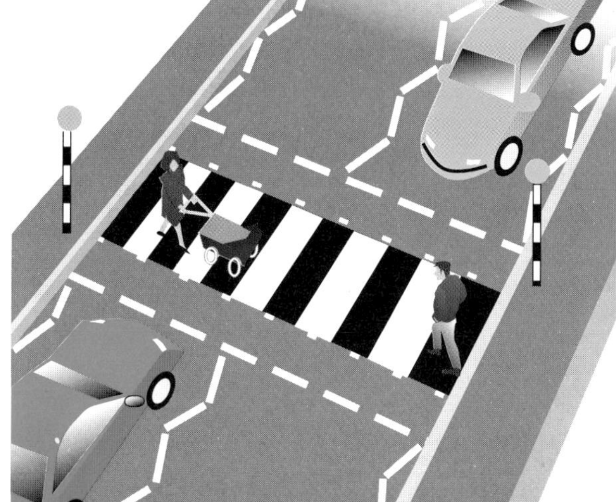

## Pelican crossings

These crossings have

- Traffic signals that change only after pedestrians have pressed a button on either side of the crossing
- A flashing amber phase to allow pedestrians already crossing to get across safely
- Zigzag lines on the road on each side of the crossing
- A stop line painted on the road for traffic waiting at the crossing

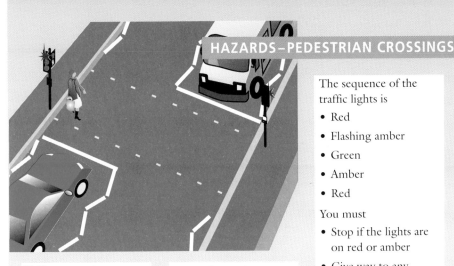

The sequence of the traffic lights is

- Red
- Flashing amber
- Green
- Amber
- Red

You must

- Stop if the lights are on red or amber
- Give way to any pedestrians crossing if the amber lights are flashing
- Give way to any pedestrians still crossing when the flashing amber light changes to green

## Puffin crossings

The term 'puffin' means pedestrian user-friendly intelligent crossings. This type of crossing has been installed at a number of selected sites and can be identified by

- Detectors sited so that the red traffic signal will be held until pedestrians have cleared the crossing
- No flashing amber phase

- Traffic lights that operate in normal sequence
  - red
  - red and amber
  - green
  - amber
  - red

You must

- Stop and wait, unless the green light is showing
- Drive over the crossing only if it's clear of pedestrians

### Toucan crossings

These crossings are mostly found in areas with college or university sites and where there are large numbers of cyclists. They operate in the same way as puffin crossings except

- Cyclists share the crossing with pedestrians without dismounting
- A green cycle light indicates when it's safe to cross

As with puffin crossings, the traffic lights operate in the normal sequence.

You must

- Stop and wait, unless the green light shows
- Drive over the crossing only if it's clear of pedestrians or cyclists

## Faults you should avoid

- Approaching any type of crossing at too high a speed
- Driving on without stopping or showing awareness of waiting pedestrians
- Driving onto or blocking a crossing
- Harassing pedestrians by
  - revving the engine
  - making the air brakes hiss
  - edging forward
  - sounding the horn
  - overtaking within the zigzag lines
  - waving pedestrians to cross

## What the test requires

When you make a normal stop you must be able to

- Select a safe place where you won't
  - – cause an obstruction
  - – create a hazard
  - – contravene any waiting, stopping or parking restrictions
- Stop reasonably close to the edge of the road

## How your examiner will test you

At times during the test the examiner will ask you to pull up either at

- A convenient place or
- A particular place, for example next to a lamp-post or, in some circumstances, at a bus stop

This is to demonstrate that you could pull up to allow passengers to board or alight safely.

The examiner will watch your driving and take account of your

- Use of the MSM/PSL routine
- Judgement in selecting a safe place to stop

## Skills you should show

You must be able to stop in a safe position by

- Selecting it in good time
- Making proper use of the MSM/PSL routine
- Only stopping where you're allowed to do so
- Not causing an obstruction
- Recognising in good time road markings or signs indicating any restriction
- Pulling up close to and parallel with the kerb
- Stopping at the correct place when asked

## Faults you should avoid

- Pulling up with insufficient warning to other road users
- Causing danger or inconvenience to any other road users
- Not complying with restrictions on
  - – waiting
  - – parking
  - – stopping
- Parking at or outside
  - – school entrances
  - – fire stations
  - – ambulance stations
  - – pedestrian crossings

## What the test requires

If you're taking a test to gain a trailer entitlement you'll be asked to uncouple and recouple your vehicle, normally at the end of the test. You should know and be able to demonstrate how to uncouple and recouple your vehicle safely.

### Uncoupling

When uncoupling you should

- Ensure that the brakes are applied on both the vehicle and trailer
- Set the jockey wheel/prop stand to support the trailer weight
- Turn off any taps, disconnect the air lines and stow the lines away safely (where fitted)
- Disconnect the electric line and stow it away safely
- Release the break-away cable connection
- Release the trailer coupling
- Drive the tractive unit away slowly, checking the trailer either directly or in the mirrors

### Recoupling

When coupling

- Ensure that the trailer brake is applied
- Reverse slowly up to the trailer
- Ensure that the vehicle parking brake is applied
- Check the height of the coupling
- Connect the tow-hitch
- Connect the break-away cable
- Connect the electric lines
- Connect the air lines and turn on taps, if fitted
- Raise the jockey wheel/prop stand
- Release the trailer parking brake
- Start up the engine
- Check that the air is building up in the storage tanks (where applicable)
- Check lights and indicators

## How your examiner will test you

Your examiner will ask you to perform this exercise where there's safe and level ground. You'll be asked to

- Demonstrate the uncoupling of your vehicle and trailer
- Pull forward until there's a gap between the vehicle and trailer
- Recouple the vehicle and trailer

Your examiner will expect you to make sure that the

- Coupling is secure
- Lights and indicators are working
- The trailer brake is released

## Skills you should show

You should be able to uncouple and recouple your vehicle and trailer

- Safely
- Confidently, and in good time
- Showing concern for your own and others' health and safety

## Faults you should avoid

### When uncoupling

- Uncoupling without applying the brakes on the towing vehicle
- Releasing the trailer coupling without the jockey wheel/prop stand being lowered
- Moving forward before the entire correct procedure has been completed

### When recoupling

- Not checking the brakes are applied on the trailer
- Not using good, effective observation of your trailer as you reverse up to it
- Leaving the towing vehicle without applying the parking brake
- Recoupling at speed

Don't attempt to move away without checking the

- Lights
- Indicators
- Trailer brake release

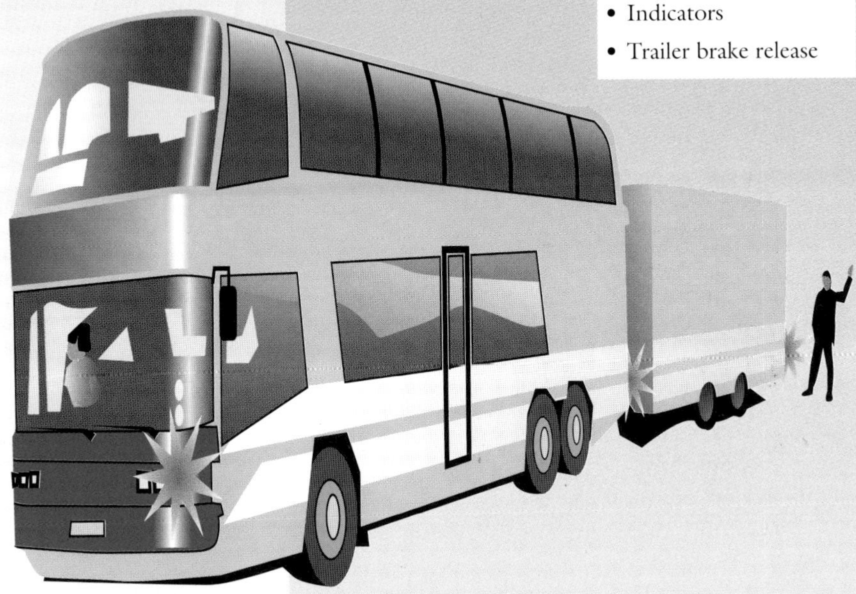

## Understanding the rules

At the end of the test the examiner will ask you to show the

- Location of the fire extinguisher
- Fuel cut-off device
- Emergency door and how it operates

With the introduction of the theory test for large goods vehicle and PCV drivers, questions on *The Highway Code* won't be asked any longer at the end of the practical driving test. However, you'll be expected to

- Put its rules into practice when you're driving
- Recognise all road signs or road markings that apply to minibus, coach or bus drivers
- Show courtesy and consideration towards all other road users

*The Highway Code* itself isn't a set of laws, rather a collection of rules offering sound guidance to all road users. Know the rules and use them whenever you drive on the road..

New road signs are introduced from time to time, and the rules set out in *The Highway Code* may be amended or increased. You should ensure that you're familiar with the most recent edition.

You should also study and be totally familiar with all the signs and road markings set out in the book *Know Your Traffic Signs* (The Stationery Office). Changes to UK traffic signs will continue to take place over a number of years. It's your responsibility to be aware of any changes as they're introduced.

## Legal requirements of the test

The candidate must show that they're competent to drive the vehicle in which the test is being conducted without danger to, and with due consideration for, other persons using the road. In particular, the candidate must show that they can competently

- Start the engine
- Move off straight ahead and at an angle
- Maintain a proper position in relation to a vehicle immediately in front
- Overtake and take an appropriate course in relation to other vehicles
- Turn right and left
- Stop within a limited distance, under full control
- Stop normally and bring the vehicle to rest in an appropriate part of the road
- Drive the vehicle forwards and backwards; whilst driving the vehicle backwards steer the vehicle along a predetermined course to make it enter a restricted opening and bring it to rest in a predetermined position
- Indicate their intended actions by appropriate signals at appropriate times
- Act correctly and promptly in response to all signals given by any traffic sign, by any person lawfully directing traffic, and by any other person using the road

## If you pass

You'll have demonstrated that you can drive a bus, coach or minibus – without passengers – to the high standard required to obtain a licence. You'll be given

- A pass certificate (D10V)
- A copy of the driving test report (DLV25A), which will show any minor faults that have been marked during the test
- A brief explanation of any minor faults marked. This is to help you to overcome any minor weaknesses in your driving as you gain experience

Answer all the questions and sign the declaration section on the back of your pass certificate and forward it (with a completed D1 form, if necessary) to the Vocational Licence Section, DVLA, Swansea SA99 1BR as soon as possible (or, in any case, within two years) to obtain full PCV licence entitlement on your driving licence.

### After you've passed

You should aim to raise your standard of driving – especially as you'll be driving buses carrying passengers.

Most operators will offer you 'type' training, which will allow you to familiarise yourself with the different vehicles on the fleet.

Your trainer should be able to give you further advice.

## If you fail

Your driving won't have been up to the high standard required to obtain the vocational driving licence. You'll have made mistakes which either caused, or could have caused, danger on the road.

Your examiner will

- Give you a statement of failure including a copy of the driving test report (DLV25A), which will show all the faults marked during the test
- Explain briefly why you've failed

You may have made mistakes that you feel were as a result of the pressure of the occasion. Remember, however, that there will frequently be times when you, as a PCV driver, will be under pressure of one sort or another. You must learn to not let it affect your driving.

You should

- Study the driving test report and refer to the relevant sections in this book
- Show your copy of the driving test report to your instructor, who will help you to correct the faults

Your instructor shouldn't concentrate solely on the faults listed, but should aim to continue to improve all aspects of your driving before you retake the test. Listen to the advice you're given and get as much practice as you can.

## Right of appeal

Although the examiner's decision can't be altered you have a right to appeal if you consider that your driving test wasn't conducted according to the regulations.

If you live in England or Wales you have six months after the issue of the statement of failure in which to appeal (Magistrates' Courts Act 1952 [Ch. 55 part VII, Section 104]). If you live in Scotland you have 21 days in which to appeal (Sheriff Court, Scotland Act of Sederunt (Statutory Appeals) 1981).

See also the DSA complaints guide for test candidates at the back of this book.

# PART SIX ADDITIONAL INFORMATION

This part offers further information that might be of help to those planning to become professional PCV drivers.

## The topics covered

- Disqualified drivers
- DSA services
- DSA Area Offices
- PCV test centres
- Traffic Area Offices
- Other useful addresses
- PCV licence entitlements
- Minimum test vehicles (MTVs)
- Vehicle types and licence requirements
- Cone positions
- Road signs
- Conclusion
- Glossary

## Retesting once disqualified

Tougher penalties now exist for anyone convicted of certain dangerous driving offences. If a driver is convicted of a dangerous driving offence, which involves a period of disqualification, all PCV entitlement is automatically lost regardless of the type of vehicle being driven at the time of the offence.

The decision about whether that entitlement can be regained is a matter for the Licensing Authority (LA). The options are

- The entitlement may be refused on the grounds that you've shown yourself to be an unfit and improper person to hold a bus or coach driving licence
- The court may require you to take an extended car driving test to regain your category B licence
- You may be required to retake a driving test for each additional category of vehicle that you want to drive
- The additional category(ies) may be restored without any further requirement, in exceptional circumstances

It's important to remember that a PCV driving licence can't be issued on its own. You must possess a valid, full driving licence entitlement for category B (a car licence) for your category D, D1 or D + E licence entitlement to be valid. If you lose your car licence entitlement you lose your PCV licence with it.

## Applying for a retest

If you have to take a category B retest you can apply for a provisional licence at the end of the period of disqualification.

The normal rules for provisional licence-holders apply

- You must be supervised by a person who's at least 21 years of age and has held (and still holds) a full licence for at least three years for the category of vehicle being driven
- L plates (or D plates, if you wish, in Wales) must be displayed to the front and rear of the vehicle
- Driving on motorways isn't allowed
- PCVs may not be driven if you've only a provisional car licence (category B)

All driving tests are booked by application to the DSA booking section at the relevant Area Office. There are higher fees for extended tests so you must make it clear when you apply which type of test you want.

You can only apply for a provisional category D licence entitlement after you've passed an extended car driving test, if the court has directed you to do so.

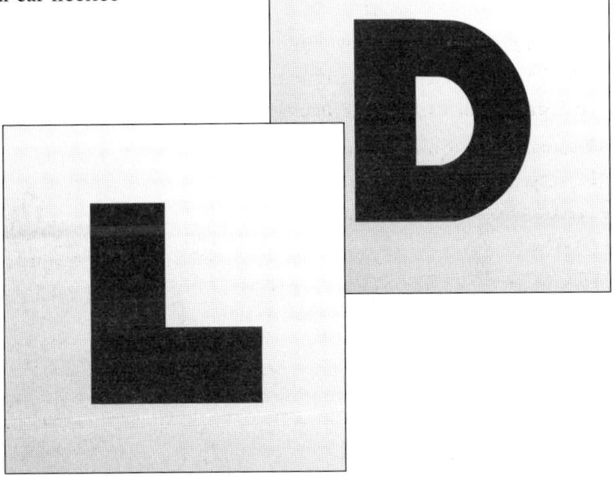

## Service standards

The Driving Standards Agency (DSA) is committed to providing a high-quality service for all its customers. If you would like information about our standards of service please contact

Customer Services Manager
Driving Standards Agency
Stanley House
Talbot Street
Nottingham
NG1 5GU

Tel: 0115 901 2515/6

## Complaints guide

DSA aims to give our customers the best possible service. Please tell us

- When we've done well
- When you aren't satisfied

Your comments can help us to improve the service that we offer.

If you have any questions about how your test was conducted please contact the local Supervising Examiner, whose address is displayed in your local driving test centre. If you're dissatisfied with the reply or wish to comment on other matters you can write to the Area Manager (see the list of Area Offices at the back of this book).

If your concern relates to an Approved Driving Instructor you should write to

The Registrar of Approved Driving Instructors
Driving Standards Agency
Stanley House
Talbot Street
Nottingham
NG1 5GU

Alternatively, you may wish to write to

The Chief Executive
Driving Standards Agency
Stanley House
Talbot Street
Nottingham
NG1 5GU

None of this removes your right to take your complaint to

- Your Member of Parliament, who may decide to raise your case personally with the DSA Chief Executive, the Minister, or the Parliamentary Commissioner for Administration (the Ombudsman), whose name and address are at the back of this book
- A magistrates court (in Scotland to the Sheriff of your area) if you believe that your test wasn't conducted in accordance with the relevant regulations

Before doing this you're advised to seek legal advice.

## Compensation code

DSA always aims to keep test appointments but occasionally tests have to be cancelled at short notice. DSA will normally refund the test fee, or give a free re-booking, in the following circumstances

- Where an appointment is cancelled by DSA – for whatever reason
- Where an appointment is cancelled by the candidate, who gives at least ten clear working days' notice
- Where the candidate keeps the test appointment, but the test doesn't take place or isn't completed for reasons not owing to the candidate or to any vehicle provided by him or her for the test

In addition, DSA will normally consider reasonable claims from the candidate for financial loss or expenditure incurred by him or her, as a result of DSA cancelling a test at short notice (other than for reasons of bad weather). For example, a claim for the commercial hire of the test vehicle will normally be considered. Applications should be made to the Area Office where the test was booked.

This compensation code doesn't affect your existing legal rights.

## DSA Head Office

Stanley House
56 Talbot Street
Nottingham
NG1 5GU

Tel: 0115 901 2500

## DSA Area Offices

DSA mail is initially processed at Newcastle. Driving tests are then booked at the DSA's five Area Offices.

### London and the South-East

DSA
PO Box 289
Newcastle-upon-Tyne
NE99 1WE

Telephone bookings by credit or debit card and other enquiries

Tel: 0171 468 4540
Fax: 0171 468 4550
Recorded message:
0171 468 4530

### Midland and Eastern

DSA
PO Box 287
Newcastle-upon-Tyne
NE99 1WB

Telephone bookings by credit or debit card and other enquiries

Tel: 0121 697 6740
Fax: 0121 697 6750
Recorded message:
0121 697 6730

### Northern

DSA
PO Box 280
Newcastle-upon-Tyne
NE99 1FP

Telephone bookings by credit or debit card and other enquiries

Tel: 0191 201 4088
Fax: 0191 201 4010
Recorded message:
0191 201 4100

### Scotland

DSA
PO Box 288
Newcastle-upon-Tyne
NE99 1WD

Telephone bookings by credit or debit card or other enquiries

Tel: 0131 529 8630
Fax: 0131 529 8630
Recorded message:
0131 529 8592

### Wales and Western

DSA
PO Box 286
Newcastle-upon-Tyne
NE99 1WA

Telephone bookings by credit or debit card and other enquiries

Tel: 0122 258 1040
Fax: 0122 258 1050
Recorded message:
0122 258 1030

**London and the South-East**

Canterbury
Croydon
Enfield
Gillingham
Guildford
Hastings
Lancing
Purfleet
Yeading

**Midlands and Eastern**

Alvaston (Derby)
Chelmsford
Culham
Featherstone (Wolverhampton)
Garrets Green (Birmingham)
Ipswich
Leicester
Leighton Buzzard
Norwich
Peterborough
Shrewsbury
Swynnerton (Stoke-on-Trent)
Waterbeach (Cambridge)
Watnall (Nottingham)
Weedon

**Northern**

Berwick*
Beverley
Bredbury (Stockport)
Carlisle
Darlington
Grimsby
Heywood (Manchester)
Keighley
Kirkham (Preston)
Leeds
Newcastle
Sheffield
Simonswood (Liverpool)
Upton (Birkenhead)
Walton (York)

**Scotland**

Aberdeen
Bishopbriggs (Glasgow)
Connel
Dumfries
Galashiels*
Inverness
Kilmarnock
Kirkwall*
Lerwick*
Livingstone (Edinburgh)
Machrihanish (Kintyre)*
Perth
Port Ellen (Islay)*
Stornoway*
Wick*

**Wales and Western**

Bristol
Caernarfon*
Camborne
Chisledon (Swindon)
Exeter
Gloucester
Isle of Wight*
Llantrisant
Llay (Wrexham)
Neath
Plymouth
Pontypool
Poole
Reading
Southampton
Taunton
Withybush (Haverfordwest)

*Tests are only conducted occasionally at these centres.

## Traffic Area Offices and Licensing Authorities

### Eastern

Terrington House
13–15 Hills Road
Cambridge CB2 1NP

Tel: 0122 335 8922

**Area covered:**
Bedfordshire
Buckinghamshire
Cambridgeshire
Essex
Hertfordshire
Leicestershire
Lincolnshire
Norfolk
Northamptonshire
Suffolk

### North-Eastern

Hillcrest House
386 Harehills Lane
Leeds LS9 6NF

Tel: 0113 283 3533

**Area covered:**
Cleveland
Durham
Humberside
North Yorkshire
Northumberland
Nottinghamshire
South Yorkshire
Tyne and Wear
West Yorkshire

### North-Western

Portcullis House
Seymour Grove
Stretford
Manchester M16 0NE

Tel: 0161 886 4000

**Area covered:**
Cheshire
Cumbria
Greater Manchester
Lancashire
Merseyside

### Scotland

Argyll House
3 Lady Lawson Street
Edinburgh EH3 9SE

Tel: 0131 529 8500

**Area covered:**
All Scotland and the Islands

### South-Eastern and Metropolitan London

Ivy House
3 Ivy Terrace
Eastbourne BN21 4QT

Tel: 0132 372 1471

**Area covered:**
East Sussex
Greater London
Kent
Surrey
West Sussex

## Wales

Caradog House
1–6 St Andrew's Place
Cardiff CF1 3PW

Tel: 01222 394 027

**Area covered:**
Clwyd
Dyfed
Glamorgan
Gwent
Gwynedd
Powys

## West Midlands

Cumberland House
200 Broad Street
Birmingham B15 1TD

Tel: 0121 608 1000

**Area covered:**
Hereford and Worcester
Shropshire
Staffordshire
Warwickshire
West Midlands

## Western

The Gaunt's House
Denmark Street
Bristol BS1 5DR

Tel: 0117 975 5000

**Area covered:**
Avon
Berkshire
Cornwall
Devon
Dorset
Gloucestershire
Hampshire
Isle of Wight
Oxfordshire
Somerset
Wiltshire

## OTHER USEFUL ADDRESSES

**Accessible Transport Group**

Greater Manchester Passenger
Transport Executive
9 Portland Street
Manchester M60 1HX

Tel: 0161 242 6243
(Minicom facility)

**British Bus Preservation Group**

The Secretary
35 Medellin Hill
Southfields
Northampton NN3 5DF

Tel: 01604 647 332

**British Road Federation**

Pillar House
194–202 Old Kent Road
London SE1 5TG

Tel: 0171 703 9769

**Bus and Coach Training Ltd**

Regency House
43 High Street
Rickmansworth
Hertfordshire WD3 1ET

Tel: 0192 389 6607

**Bus and Coach Working Group (DiPTAC)**

The DOT Mobility Unit
111 Great Minster House
76 Marsham Street
London SW1P 4DR

Tel: 0171 271 5258

**CENTREX**
**Road Transport Industry Training and Business Services Ltd**

MOTEC Telford
High Ercall
Telford TF6 6RB

Tel: 01952 777 777
Fax: 01952 777 799

**Chartered Institute of Transport**

80 Portland Place
London W1N 4DP

Tel: 0171 636 9952

**City and Guilds of London Institute**

1 Giltspur Street
London EC1A 9DD

Tel: 0171 294 2468

**Coach Operators' Federation**

261 Stowey Road
Yatton
Bristol BS19 4QX

Tel: 0193 483 2074

**Community Transport Association**

Highbank
Halton Street
Hyde
Cheshire SK14 2NY

Tel & Fax: 0161 366 6685
Tel & Fax: 0161 351 1475

**Confederation of Passenger Transport UK**

(previously the Bus and Coach Council)
Imperial House
15–19 Kingsway
London WC2B 6UN

Tel: 0171 240 3131
Fax: 0171 240 6565

**Department of Transport Mobility Advice and Vehicle Information Service (MAVIS)**

'O' Wing, Macadam Avenue
Old Wokingham Road
Crowthorne RG45 6XD

Tel: 0134 477 0456
Fax: 0134 466 1066

**Driver and Vehicle Licensing Agency (DVLA) Customer Enquiry Unit**

Swansea SA6 7JL

Tel: 0179 277 2151
Minicom: 0179 278 2756
Fax: 0179 278 3071
(Ring between 8.15 and 4.30 Monday–Friday)

**DVLA Drivers' Medical Branch**

Swansea SA99 1TU

Tel: 0179 230 4000

**DVLA The Vocational Licence Centre**

Swansea SA99 1BR

Tel: 01792 772 151

**Health and Safety Executive Agency**

Enquiry Unit
Broad Lane
Sheffield S3 7HQ

Tel: 0541 545 500
(See your telephone book for details of your area HSE office.)

**Historic Commercial Vehicle Society**

Iden Grange
Cranbrook Road
Staplehurst
Kent TN12 0ET

Fax: 0158 089 3227

**London Regional Passengers' Committee**

Clements House
14/18 Gresham Street
London EC2V 7PR

Tel: 0171 505 9000

**Metropolitan Police Coach Advisory Service**

Traffic Headquarters
New Scotland Yard
Broadway
London SW1H 0BG

Tel: 0171 230 3072

**National Federation of Bus Users**

PO Box 320
Portsmouth PO5 3SD

Tel: 0170 581 4493

# OTHER USEFUL ADDRESSES

**National Playbus Association**

93 Whitby Road
Brislington
Bristol BS4 3QF

Tel: 0117 977 5375

**Parliamentary Commissioner for Administration (The Ombudsman)**

W K Reid CB
Church House
Great Smith Street
London SW1P 3BW

Tel: 0171 276 2003/3000

**The Road Operator's Safety Council**

395 Cowley Road
Oxford OX4 2DJ

Tel: 01865 775 552

**Royal Society for the Prevention of Accidents (RoSPA)**

353 Bristol Road
Birmingham B5 7ST

Tel: 0121 248 2000

**Traffic Director for London**

College House
Great Peter Street
London SW1P 3LN

Tel: 0171 222 4545
Fax: 0171 976 8640

The licence entitlements you'll require to drive different types of buses, coaches and minibuses are listed here. You must hold full (not provisional) category B entitlement before you can take a test in this group. You must also gain a full category entitlement for a vehicle before taking a second test to add the trailer entitlement (+ E). No additional entitlement is required to tow trailers that weigh less than 750kg.

| Category | Description | Additional categories covered |
|---|---|---|
| D | Any bus with more than 8 passenger seats | D1 |
| D1 | Buses with 9–16 passenger seats | None |
| D + E | Articulated buses and buses towing trailers over 750kg | D, D1, D1 + E |
| D1 + E | Buses with 9–16 passenger seats towing trailers over 750kg, provided the combination doesn't exceed 12 tonnes and the laden trailer weight doesn't exceed the unladen weight of the towing vehicle | D1 |

Articulated or 'bendi-buses' may be driven on a category D licence.

If the vehicle you use for your driving test has automatic transmission your licence entitlement won't include vehicles with manual gearboxes. A vehicle with automatic transmission is defined as a vehicle in which the driver isn't provided with any means whereby he or she may, independently of the use of the accelerator or the brakes, vary the proportion of the power being produced by the engine that's transmitted to the road wheels of the vehicle. This definition includes semi-automatic vehicles, where no clutch pedal exists.

Minibuses may be driven with a category B licence entitlement within the UK only provided

- The vehicle is used by a non-commercial body for social purposes only
- The driver is 21 years or more and has held a full car licence for at least two years
- The driver provides his or her services on a voluntary (unpaid) basis
- The minibus weighs no more than 3.5 tonnes (or 4.25 tonnes if specially adapted for disabled passengers)

All test vehicles in this group must be capable of 80 kph (50 mph).

| Licence category | Minimum specification of vehicle |
|---|---|
| D | Any PCV with more than 8 passenger seats and at least 9 metres (29 feet 3 in.) long |
| D1 | Any PCV with 9–16 passenger seats* |
| + E (Towing trailers) | If you want an entitlement to tow a trailer over 750kg behind a bus in one of the above categories, you must tow a trailer with a maximum authorised mass (MAM) of at least 1,250kg behind the vehicle you use throughout the driving test. You must have passed a driving test using such a vehicle without a trailer before you can take this additional test. If you already have a C + E entitlement this requirement is waived. |

***Important note** A vehicle with more than 17 seats, including the driver's, isn't suitable for category D1. A vehicle must fall within the category or sub-category for which the licence is being sought **in addition to meeting the MTV specification.**

You should check with the DVLA if you're in any doubt as to the licence entitlement that you require. After 1 January 1997 the entitlement you'll need for the types of vehicles listed in this book are as follows.

| Type of vehicle | Category required | Notes |
|---|---|---|
| Small minibus with fewer than 9 passenger seats | B | May be subject to taxi or private hire vehicle regulations if used commercially |
| Minibus or midibus with 9–16 passenger seats | D1 | D1 allows passengers to be carried for hire or reward |
| Single-decker service bus or midibus with more than 16 passenger seats | D | |
| Coaches with more than 16 passenger seats | D | |
| Buses towing trailers over 750kg | D + E | |
| 'Supertrams' | B | Further qualifications are required to comply with the light rail transit (LRT) systems regulations |
| Double-decker service buses and coaches (including those with 3 or 4 axles) | D | |
| Historic buses and coaches, i.e., vehicles over 30 years old | D | In some cases these may be driven with category B entitlement – when not being used for hire or reward, or the carriage of more than 8 passengers |
| Mobile project and playbuses | C | In some cases these may be driven with category B entitlement |
| Towing trailers | + E | In addition to the vehicle category |

## Ready reckoner: metric measurements

This list of metric measurements should prove useful if you want to practise the reversing exercise.

To calculate the reversing area's layout identify the length of your vehicle in the left-hand columns and scan across to the right-hand columns for the relevant cone measurements. The cone positions are relative to the base line Z (see diagram on p. 170).

| Metres | Feet | Cone A | Cone B |
|---|---|---|---|
| 4.50 | 14.8 | 22.5 | 13.5 |
| 4.75 | 15.6 | 23.8 | 14.3 |
| 5.00 | 16.4 | 25.0 | 15.0 |
| 5.25 | 17.2 | 26.3 | 15.8 |
| 5.50 | 18.0 | 27.5 | 16.5 |
| 5.75 | 18.9 | 28.8 | 17.3 |
| 6.00 | 19.7 | 30.0 | 18.0 |
| 6.25 | 20.5 | 31.3 | 18.8 |
| 6.50 | 21.3 | 32.5 | 19.5 |
| 6.75 | 22.1 | 33.8 | 20.3 |
| 7.00 | 23.0 | 35.0 | 21.0 |
| 7.25 | 23.8 | 36.3 | 21.8 |
| 7.50 | 24.6 | 37.5 | 22.5 |
| 7.75 | 25.4 | 38.8 | 23.3 |
| 8.00 | 26.2 | 40.0 | 24.0 |
| 8.25 | 27.1 | 41.3 | 24.8 |
| 8.50 | 27.9 | 42.5 | 25.5 |
| 8.75 | 28.7 | 43.8 | 26.3 |
| 9.00 | 29.5 | 45.0 | 27.0 |
| 9.25 | 30.3 | 46.3 | 27.8 |
| 9.50 | 31.2 | 47.5 | 28.5 |
| 9.75 | 32.0 | 48.8 | 29.3 |
| 10.00 | 32.8 | 50.0 | 30.0 |
| 10.25 | 33.6 | 51.3 | 30.8 |
| 10.50 | 34.4 | 52.5 | 31.5 |
| 10.75 | 35.3 | 53.8 | 32.3 |
| 11.00 | 36.1 | 55.0 | 33.0 |
| 11.25 | 36.9 | 56.3 | 33.8 |
| 11.50 | 37.7 | 57.5 | 34.5 |
| 11.75 | 38.5 | 58.8 | 35.3 |
| 12.00 | 39.4 | 60.0 | 36.0 |
| 12.25 | 40.2 | 61.3 | 36.8 |
| 12.50 | 41.0 | 62.5 | 37.5 |
| 12.75 | 41.8 | 63.8 | 38.3 |
| 13.00 | 42.7 | 65.0 | 39.0 |
| 13.25 | 43.5 | 66.3 | 39.8 |
| 13.50 | 44.3 | 67.5 | 40.5 |
| 13.75 | 45.1 | 68.8 | 41.3 |
| 14.00 | 45.9 | 70.0 | 42.0 |
| 14.25 | 46.8 | 71.3 | 42.8 |
| 14.50 | 47.6 | 72.5 | 43.5 |
| 14.75 | 48.4 | 73.8 | 44.3 |
| 15.00 | 49.2 | 75.0 | 45.0 |
| 15.25 | 50.0 | 76.3 | 45.8 |
| 15.50 | 50.9 | 77.5 | 46.5 |
| 15.75 | 51.7 | 78.8 | 47.3 |
| 16.00 | 52.5 | 80.0 | 48.0 |
| 16.25 | 53.3 | 81.3 | 48.8 |
| 16.50 | 54.1 | 82.5 | 49.5 |
| 16.75 | 55.0 | 83.8 | 50.3 |
| 17.00 | 55.8 | 85.0 | 51.0 |
| 17.25 | 56.6 | 86.3 | 51.8 |
| 17.50 | 57.4 | 87.5 | 52.5 |
| 17.75 | 58.2 | 88.8 | 53.3 |
| 18.00 | 59.1 | 90.0 | 54.0 |
| 18.25 | 59.9 | 91.3 | 54.8 |

You must be aware of the specific road signs that relate to buses and coaches. Those illustrated on this page are currently in use.

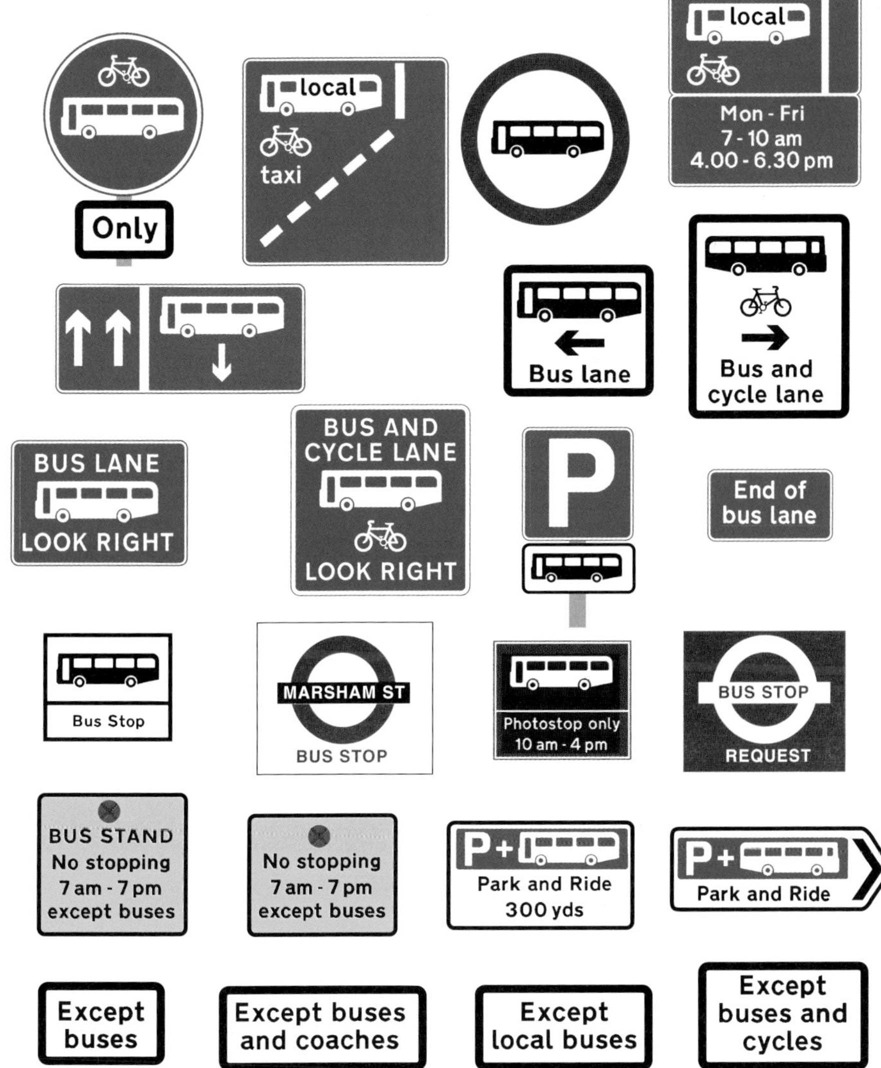

Buses, coaches, minibuses and trams have developed rapidly over the past decade or so. Modern vehicles are fitted with 'smart engines' and 'thinking gearboxes', and the driver is surrounded by all manner of electronic circuitry to make the job easier, less stressful and often very enjoyable. The manufacturers have listened to the needs of drivers, passengers and operators equally when designing their products.

Today's bus driver should have 'service to the customer' as a primary aim. However, to give a professional service you need to be a skilled, dedicated driver – your driving should be to the highest standards. Your vehicle has made that easier, but the responsibilities you have are greater than they've ever been.

It's in your own interest to keep up to date with changes in requirements as they occur. Ignorance is no defence in law. Read the informative articles that appear in magazines devoted to driving. Remember, by passing the PCV driving test you'll only just be setting out on your career. Driving is a life skill that needs constant practice and revision.

If you've read this book because you drive a vehicle that doesn't require you to take a test, or if you took yours some time ago, you've already shown that you understand the need for high standards in your driving. If you're a 'bus enthusiast' you'll find you enjoy your interest more if your depth of knowledge and understanding has been increased. Whatever your reason, by studying this book you'll have made your objective

**Safe driving for life.**

A **ABS** Anti-lock braking system (developed by Bosch) that uses electronic sensors to detect when a wheel is about to lock, releases the brakes sufficiently to allow the wheel to revolve, then repeats the process in a very short space of time – thus reducing the risk of skidding.

**AETR rules** European agreement concerning the work of crews on vehicles engaged in international road transport (aligned with EU regulations in April 1992). These rules govern drivers' hours and rest periods in specified countries outside the EU. For more detailed information please consult PSV375, published by the Department of Transport.

**Air suspension system** This uses a compressible material (usually air), contained in chambers located between the axle and the vehicle body, to replace normal steel-leaf spring suspension. Gives even height (empty or laden) and added comfort to passengers. It's also known as 'road-friendly' suspension.

**Axle weights** Limits laid down for maximum permitted weights carried by each axle.

B **BS 5750** British Standards code relating to quality assurance adopted by vehicle body-builders, recovery firms, etc.

C **C & U (Regs)** Construction and Use regulations that govern the design and use of passenger vehicles.

**CAG** Computer-aided gearshift system, developed by Scania, that employs an electronic control unit combined with electropneumatic actuators and a mechanical gearbox. The clutch is still required to achieve the gear change using an electrical gear lever switch.

**COSHH Regulations 1988** The Control of Substances Hazardous to Health Regulations 1988 place a responsibility on employers to make a proper assessment of the effects of the storage or use of any substances that may represent a risk to their employees' health. Details can be obtained from the Health and Safety Executive.

**CPC** Certificate of Professional Competence indicates that the holder has attained the standards of knowledge required in order to exercise proper control of a transport business (required before an operator's licence can be granted).

**Cruise control** A facility that allows a vehicle to travel at a set speed without use of the accelerator pedal. However, the driver can immediately return to normal control by pressing the accelerator or brake pedal. This is rarely fitted to large PCVs but may be found on some minibuses.

D **Diff-lock** A device by which the driver can arrange for the power to be transmitted to both wheels on an axle (normally rotating at different speeds when the vehicle is cornering, for example), which increases traction on surfaces such as mud, snow, etc.

**DiPTAC (Disabled Persons Transport Advisory Committee) specification** Applied to PCVs to assist passengers with disabilities (for example, bright yellow handrails, etc.).

**Double de-clutching** A technique employed when driving older PCVs that allows the driver to adjust the engine revs to the road speed when changing gear. The clutch pedal is released briefly while the gear lever is in the neutral position. When changing down, engine revs are increased to match the engine speed to the lower gear in order to minimise the load being placed on the gear mechanism.
**Note:** The construction of modern synchromesh gearboxes is such that this technique can cause damage. At least one major manufacturer has made it clear that the warranty conditions will become invalid if this technique has been used. Refer to the manufacturer and the vehicle handbook, if in doubt.

**Drive-by-wire** Modern electronic and air control systems that replace direct mechanical linkages.

E **Electronic engine management system** This system monitors and controls both fuel supply to the engine and the contents of the exhaust gases produced. The system is an essential part of some speed-retarder systems.

**Electronic power shift** A semi-automatic transmission system that requires the clutch to be fully depressed each time a gear change is made. The system then selects the appropriate gear.

**Endurance braking** *See* Retarder.

F **Fluid flywheel** Incorporated in automatic and semi-automatic gear systems, it couples the drive train to the gearbox by use of hydraulic fluid. This allows gear changes, stopping and starting without the need for a separate clutch.

G **Geartronic** A fully automated transmission system developed by Volvo. There's no clutch pedal, but an additional pedal operating an exhaust brake instead.

**GVW** Gross vehicle weight, applying to vehicles that include fuel, passengers, etc.

H **HSE** The Health and Safety Executive. The HSE produce literature that provides advice and information on health and safety issues at work.

J **Jake brake** A long-established system of speed retarding that alters the valve timing in the engine. In effect, the engine becomes a compressor and holds back the vehicle's speed.

K **Kerb weight** The total weight of a vehicle plus fuel, excluding any load (or driver).

**'Kneeling' bus** This type of bus uses air suspension to lower the entrance of the bus, whilst stationary, for easier access – especially useful for disabled passengers.

L **LA** The Licensing Authority, which is an official appointed to act on behalf of the Traffic Commissioners for a Traffic Area.

**Laminated** A process whereby plastic film is sandwiched between two layers of glass so that an object upon striking a windscreen, for example, will normally chip or craze the screen without large fragments of glass causing injury to the driver.

**Limited-stop service** A bus service operating under stage carriage conditions, but stopping only at specified points.

**LNG** Liquefied (compressed) Natural Gas.

**Load-sensing valve** A valve in an air brake system that can be adjusted to reduce the possibility of wheels locking when the vehicle is unladen.

**LPG** Liquefied (compressed) Petroleum Gas.

P **Plated** A plate fixed to the vehicle with information relating to dimensions and weights of passenger vehicles. It indicates tyre size, maximum axle weight and maximum loaded weight. Certificates are sometimes referred to as 'plates' when required, with information relating to tachographs, speed limiters, manufacturer's specifications and height.

**Pneumo-cyclic gearbox** A semi-automatic gearbox, where an electronic or mechanical gearshift operates an air valve system to change gears.

**Pre-selector gearbox** A gear-change system where the gears are manually selected prior to use and then engaged by pressing a gear-change pedal. It employs a fluid flywheel and no clutch.

R **Range change** A gearbox arrangement that permits the driver to select a series of either high or low ratio gears depending on the load, speed and any gradient being negotiated. Rarely fitted to PCVs.

**Red Routes** Approximately 300 route miles in the London area are becoming subject to stringent regulations restricting stopping, unloading and loading.

**Re-grooving** A process permitted for use on tyres for vehicles over an unladen weight of 2,540kg, allowing a new tread pattern to be cut into the existing tyre surface (subject to certain conditions).

**Retarder or endurance brake** An additional braking system that may be either mechanical or electrical. Mechanical devices either alter the engine exhaust gas flow or amend the valve timing (creating a 'compressor' effect). Electrical devices comprise an electromagnetic field energised around the transmission drive shaft (most frequently used on passenger vehicles). This type may also be known as 'regenerative' braking, when the energy generated is fed back into the vehicle's electrical storage system (batteries).

S **Semi-automatic** A transmission system in which there's no clutch but the driver changes gear manually.

**Skip change** Also known as block change, this sequence of gear-changing omits intermediate gears. Sometimes referred to as 'selective' gear-changing.

**Splitter box** Another name for a gearbox with high and low ratios.

**Stage carriage service** A local bus service operating according to a route timetable and charging fares based on 'stages' of the journey.

T **Tachograph** A recorder indicating vehicle speeds, duration of journey, rest stops, etc. Required to be fitted to specified vehicles.

**TBV** Initials of the French (Renault) semi-automatic transmission system that employs a selector lever plus visual display information.

**Thinking gearbox** A term used to describe a fully automated gearbox that selects the appropriate gear for the load, gradient and speed, etc. by means of electronic sensors.

**Toughened safety glass** The glass undergoes a heat treatment process during manufacture so that in the event of an impact on the windscreen (a stone, etc.) it breaks up into small blunt fragments, thus reducing the risk of injury. An area in front of the driver is designed to give a zone of vision in the event of an impact.

**Turbo-charged** Forced air (from an exhaust-driven fan) mixed with fuel to give increased engine performance.

**Turbo-cooled** Forced air (fan-driven) in addition to liquid engine coolant. Also referred to as 'intercooling'.

**Two-speed axle** An electrical switch actuates a mechanism in the rear axle that doubles the number of ratios available to the driver.

U **Unloader valve** A device fitted to air brake systems, between the compressor and the storage reservoir, pre-set to operate when sufficient pressure is achieved and allowing the excess air to be released (often heard at regular intervals when the engine is running).

V **VED** Vehicle excise duty or the road fund licence.

Printed in the United Kingdom for The Stationery Office
N0022175 C80 6/97